—— Making History ——

Struggles for Power

Britain 1300–1700

John Patrick

Formerly Lecturer in History
Aberdeen College of Education

Mollie Packham

Formerly Head of History
Falmer School, Brighton

Illustrations by Susan Bird

John Murray

Making History

Already published in this series

The Age of Invasions: Britain 55 BC–AD 1200

In preparation

The Age of Empire: The British Overseas, 1700–1900
Years of Change: Britain 1700–1980
The Twentieth-Century World

Acknowledgements

The authors and publisher would like to thank the following for their help and advice: Mr T. Framrose, Head of Readers' Services, Sussex University; Ms Jeannette Richardson, Hove Reference Library, Sussex.

Particular thanks are due to Dr Martin Booth of Cambridge University Department of Education, for his help in the preparation of this series.

Thanks are also due to the following for permission to reproduce copyright photographs:
pp. 9, 69 (and cover), 123 (and cover), reproduced by gracious permission of Her Majesty Queen Elizabeth II; p. 13, Welsh Tourist Board; p. 15, the Dean and Chapter of Westminster; pp. 17, 18, Scottish Tourist Board; p. 19, the Keeper of the Records of Scotland; pp. 20, 38, 44, 76, John Patrick; pp. 22, 24, 37, 40, 49, 51 (right, and cover), 56, British Library; p. 28, B. T. Batsford Ltd; p. 32, the Essex County Archivist; p. 42, Bibliothèque Royale Albert 1er, Brussels; p. 51 (left), National Gallery; pp. 55, 57, 62, 72, 101, 104, 106, 132, 136, National Portrait Gallery; p. 60, the Controller, HMSO (Crown Copyright); pp. 66, 102, Ashmolean Museum, Oxford; pp. 63, 91, 117, 124, 126, British Museum; pp. 67, 105, National Buildings Record; p. 77 (top, and cover) Welsh Office; p. 77 (bottom) Victoria and Albert Museum; pp. 95, 119, the Master and Fellows, Magdalene College, Cambridge University; pp. 96, 135, Science Museum; pp. 110 (and cover), 111, National Maritime Museum; p. 113 (and cover), the Marquess of Tavistock and the trustees of the Bedford Estates; p. 118, Museum of London; p. 127, Rijksmuseum, Amsterdam; p. 134, Wellcome Institute Library; p. 141, Guildhall Library.

In addition, thanks are due to the Ordnance Survey (Crown copyright reserved) for permission to adapt from their sources the illustration on p. 43.

The authors and publisher are grateful to the following for permission to reproduce copyright material: pp. 41, 45, Penguin Classics, *Piers Plowman*; p. 135, Mae and Ira Freeman, *Fun with Science*, Kaye & Ward, London.

First published 1986
by John Murray (Publishers) Ltd
50 Albemarle Street, London W1X 4BD

Typeset by Fakenham Photosetting Ltd
Printed and bound in Great Britain
at The Bath Press, Avon

British Library Cataloguing in Publication Data
Patrick, John, 1931–
   Struggles for power: Britain 1300–1700.
   1. Great Britain—Politics and government
   I. Title   II. Packham, Mollie   III. Series
320.941   JN137
   ISBN 0-7195-4231-6

Contents

Introduction

The *Making History* series does not set out to provide a continuous narrative covering the whole of British history. Instead it aims to study the history of Britain in the context of the wider world. It emphasises both the links which, throughout its history, have bound Britain to other countries, and the multicultural heritage of the British people.

Each of the first three books in the series has five main units linked by a broad common theme. Each unit explores selected aspects of British life during a particular period, bringing it to life in a way that would be impossible in a general survey.

Struggles for Power, the second book in the series, begins with a study of feudalism and kingship, moves on to the Reformation and the age of exploration and discovery, and finishes with seventeenth-century London and the end of the Stuarts. Each of the main units follows the same basic pattern, opening with the vividly told story of an incident. This sets the scene for the whole unit, and is followed by a structured sequence of carefully graded exercises and activities. These lead to further sequences of text and closely integrated study sections, which are centred on the text, but also expand the themes and ideas contained in the text and introduce new material.

The *Inquiry* takes as its theme the religious upheavals of the sixteenth century, and the arrival of the Huguenots in England. Pupils are provided with a wide range of evidence and are encouraged to evaluate it, and come to their own conclusions. The *Topic work* that ends the book provides an opportunity to follow up some of the themes running through the book in more detail, and offers guidance on how to find and present material. Both this section and the *Inquiry* will help to further the development of historical skills and the ability to carry out independent research.

It is hoped that pupils who use the first three volumes in the series, and who continue to study history, will acquire the skills they need to approach examination work with confidence; and that those who then cease to study the subject will have formed a coherent view of the making of the British people, and gained some insight into the way history is written.

A note about money

In the Middle Ages the value of money depended on how much gold or silver the coins contained.
240 silver pennies weighed a pound, and so were called a 'pound'.

On bills and accounts 12 pence were called a shilling, but there were no shilling coins until 1503. There were 20 shillings in a pound.
Prices and wages have been left in pounds, shillings and pence.
The shilling has now become our 5p piece.

Average wages and prices 1300–1700 (in old pence)

An agricultural labourer's daily pay	Year	The price of a loaf of bread weighing 4 lb (2 kg)
2 pence	1300	1 penny
4 pence	1400	1 penny
4 pence	1500	1 penny
10 pence	1600	5 pence
12 pence	1700	6.5 pence

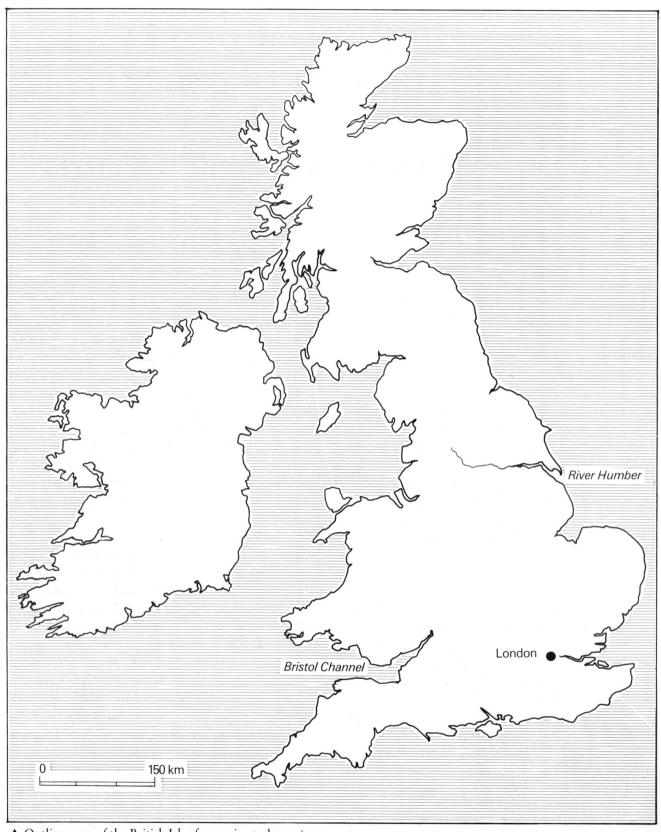

River Humber

Bristol Channel

London ●

0   150 km

▲ Outline map of the British Isles for use in study sections

1 Conquest and War in Britain and France

William Wallace and the Sheriff of Lanark

In 1297 the English ruled Scotland. Edward I's army had conquered the country a year earlier, and he had appointed English sheriffs to govern it. In the town of Lanark the sheriff was Sir William Hazelrigg, and he had brought English soldiers and officials to help govern the area.

Sunday morning in Lanark
It was a fine Sunday in spring, and the congregation were just leaving Lanark church after Mass. Most of them were poor people, plainly dressed in drab clothes made of coarse, cheap cloth. But among them there was a small group of young men who stood out from the rest. They wore well-cut suits of fine green cloth. They had swords at their belts and one of them, William Wallace, younger son of Sir Malcolm Wallace of Elderslie, also carried a small jewelled dagger.

A fight breaks out
As they walked towards the town centre the young men passed an Englishman who was standing enjoying the spring sunshine. He began to tease them. First he greeted them in French because, he said, he thought that anyone wearing such splendid clothes must be foreign. When they replied that they were Scots he asked, 'What do you think you are doing wearing these fine clothes?' Then he caught sight of Wallace's dagger and asked him, 'What right have you to carry such a valuable knife?'

Wallace and his friends grew angry and shouted back at him. Hearing the noise, a number of English soldiers came out of nearby houses. They told the Scots to move on, and began to try to push them along. The Scots refused to move and drew their swords. A real fight began.

The Scots won. They killed a number of English soldiers and the rest ran for shelter in the alleys and houses of the town.

The search for Wallace
Wallace knew that as soon as the sheriff heard of the fight he would send out a party to search for all the Scots who had dared to kill his soldiers. So he hurried home, changed his clothes, and went to hide in the woods on the outskirts of the town.

A couple of hours later English troops burst into Wallace's house. They searched it from top to bottom, and when they were certain that Wallace was not there, they arrested his wife instead and took her to Hazelrigg, the sheriff.

The death of Wallace's wife
Hazelrigg immediately asked Marion Wallace where her husband was hiding. She refused to say. Hazelrigg was furious and threatened her with his sword. She still refused to speak, and in his rage, Hazelrigg stabbed and killed her.

As dusk fell that evening one of Wallace's servants made her way out of the town and up into the woods where Wallace and his friends were hiding. She told them what had happened. The news seemed to shatter Wallace's men. At first they could hardly believe it. Then they sat and wept.

Wallace himself roused them to action. 'All this weeping is pointless,' he said. 'It cannot bring her back to life. Let us instead think of revenge. Ten thousand men shall die to pay for her life.'

Wallace's revenge
At dead of night Wallace and his men made their way down to the town. They moved

quietly through the streets until they reached the house where the sheriff was lying asleep. The door was locked and barred, but Wallace burst it off its hinges and crashed into the house.

With his sword in his hand he bounded up the stairs to the top of the house where Hazelrigg had his bedroom. He flung open the door, and found the sheriff, who had been woken by the noise, sitting up in bed.

'What is the meaning of all this din?' shouted Hazelrigg. 'And who are you to come rampaging into my room like a madman?' Wallace answered, 'I am William Wallace whom you have been looking for all day, and I have come to make sure that you pay dearly for the life of the woman whom you killed.'

He strode to the bed, raised his sword and with a single blow split Sir William's head in two. Then he turned and left the room. He made his way down into the street where his men were setting fire to all the houses where Englishmen were living. As the panic-stricken men came running out the Scots killed them.

The English leave Lanark
By morning there was not a single English person left in Lanark. All the soldiers had been killed. The women, priests and a few officials had left the town. They had promised that if they were allowed to leave they would never return. On this condition the Scots let them go unharmed.

The fame of Wallace
Wallace's adventures in Lanark made him famous all over the country. The English offered a reward for his capture, dead or alive. To the Scots he was a hero—exactly the kind of man they needed to lead them in their struggle to drive the English out of their country.

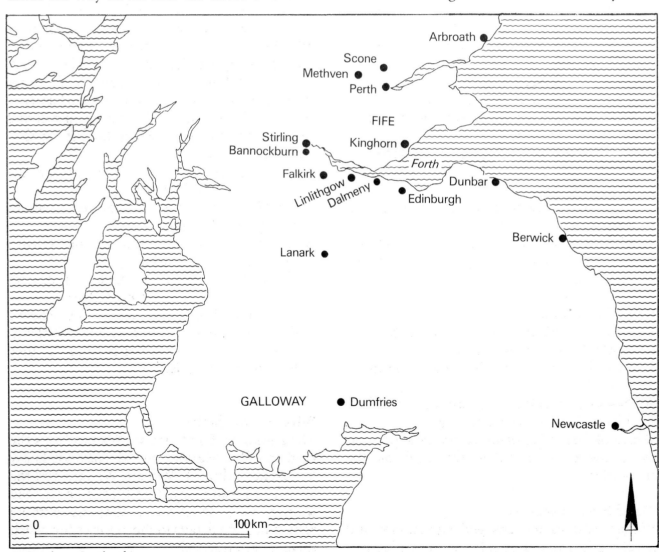

▲ Southern Scotland in 1300

Studying the story

How do we know?

Wallace's trial

William Wallace was captured by the English in 1305 and put on trial in the Great Hall at Westminster. When the charges against him were read out, the murder of Sheriff Hazelrigg was first on the list. We still have this list today, but we do not have any evidence from the trial to show *why* Wallace committed the murder.

Monks' chronicles

The *Fordun Chronicle* says that 'Wallace lifted up his head and killed the sheriff'.

The *Lanercost Chronicle* states that two Scottish noblemen tried to start a rebellion against King Edward. When they failed, they needed someone to do their work for them, so they 'caused a certain bloody man, William Wallace, who had been a chief of brigands in Scotland, to revolt against the King'.

1 When Wallace was tried, what was the first crime he was charged with?

2 Have we any evidence from the trial to show *why* he may have killed Hazelrigg?

3 Which chronicle
(a) supports the charge made at the trial that Wallace killed Hazelrigg?
(b) says that when Wallace began his rebellion he was working for two Scottish noblemen?

What do you think?

The story of 'William Wallace and the Sheriff of Lanark' tells us that Wallace:

(i) Rebelled and killed the King's sheriff in Lanark.

(ii) Began his rebellion because the sheriff had killed his wife, Marion.

Which of these statements *cannot* be supported by evidence from either the trial or the chronicles?

'Blind Harry's Wallace'

William Wallace was charged with treason and executed in 1305. Roughly 200 years later, a poem about him appeared in Scotland. It told Wallace's life-story, and described how he began a rebellion because the English first picked a quarrel with him and then killed his wife when she would not tell them where he was hiding. The writer of the poem said the English had done nothing but harm to the Scots, and his Scottish readers agreed with him.

The author gave his name as Henry the Minstrel. The Scots thought he was a poor blind man, and believed him when he claimed that the information for his poem came from an old book written by one of Wallace's followers. They included his stories in their history books.

Historians today say that he was not blind at all. They think that he was a writer who knew what the people at that time would like to read. Some of the things he tells us about Wallace are true but a great deal is made up. This story is based on 'Blind Harry's Wallace'. You will find many good stories in history books but they may not all be true.

1 (a) Why did the Scots call Henry the Minstrel, 'Blind Harry'?
(b) What do historians today believe about Henry the Minstrel?

2 (a) What was the author of the poem's opinion of the English?
(b) Why did many of his readers agree with him after they had read his poem?

3 For hundreds of years many Scots believed that the stories in 'Blind Harry's Wallace' were true. What reason or reasons did they have to believe this?

What do you think?

The author of 'Blind Harry's Wallace' says the English killed Marion, but he does not know how. The author of 'William Wallace and the Sheriff of Lanark' says that Hazelrigg stabbed Marion in a fit of rage. Why do authors sometimes add details to their stories for which there is no evidence?

→

Understanding what happened

The events listed below are all mentioned in the story of 'William Wallace and the Sheriff of Lanark'. Four of them really happened but we think that Blind Harry made up the rest. Copy out the events that you think really happened.

1 In 1296 King Edward of England invaded Scotland.

2 Scotland was governed by English sheriffs and their soldiers.

3 An English soldier picked a quarrel with Wallace and his friends as they were leaving Lanark church.

4 Wallace and his men hid because they killed some English soldiers.

5 Sheriff Hazelrigg killed Marion because she would not tell him where her husband was hiding.

6 Wallace killed Sheriff Hazelrigg and drove the English out of Lanark.

7 The English offered a reward for Wallace, dead or alive.

What do you think?
Why do the Scots still think that Wallace is a hero, even though they know that much of what Blind Harry wrote about him is not true?

▲ The Englishman jeers at Wallace and his men

Further work

Writing

1. Write the report that an English official might have sent to King Edward following the day of violence in Lanark.

   Things to write about:

   An account of the sheriff's murder and the massacre of the English soldiers,

   A report on the condition of English survivors,

   A statement about the condition of the town of Lanark after the revolt.

2. Blind Harry describes his hero, Wallace, as well-built, good-looking and scarred from old battle wounds. Write a description of
   (a) the heroine, Marion,
   (b) the villain, Hazelrigg, as you imagine him from reading the story.

3. Write an account of the quarrel outside the church in such a way that the reader sympathises with the English soldier and his comrades.

Drawing

1. (a) Draw the map of southern Scotland on page 2.
   (b) Write a sentence under your drawing explaining what English soldiers were doing in Scotland in 1296.

2. The English government offered a reward for Wallace, dead or alive. Draw a 'Wanted' poster

   showing a picture of Wallace,

   describing the crime he committed,

   promising a large reward.

3. Design a book cover for a modern edition of 'Blind Harry's Wallace'. Write a brief account that might be written on the inside of the jacket, giving the reader an idea of the kind of book to expect.

Drama and oral work

1. Divide into groups of five.
2. Divide the story into five or six sections and give one section to each group.
3. In your group, divide the section of reading between you and think of some suitable sound effects, for example, the wind moaning in the trees of the forest at dusk. Give everyone fifteen minutes to practise the reading and sound effects.
4. Perform the reading as a class. If it is good enough, make a tape recording.

Making a history glossary

A history glossary is a collection of words that you need to use and understand when you study history. In Book 1 of this series you were given a glossary. Now you can make your own.

1. Take a double page, either in the middle or at the end of your book, and set it out as shown here:

2. Begin your glossary by writing *sheriff* in the first Word column.
3. In the first Meaning column, explain, in your own words, the meaning of the word sheriff.
4. Find out what a *chronicle* is, and write it down in your glossary.

History glossary			
Word	Meaning	Word	Meaning

The power of King Edward

King Edward I, who invaded Scotland in 1296, was King of England from 1272 to 1307. He was tall, strong and energetic. He enjoyed commanding armies in battle, and knew more about war than any other king of his day.

Land and power

To fight a war Edward needed men and money. To get them, he rented out land to tenants. In return, the tenants had to pay taxes and serve in his army. So Edward's wealth and power depended on the amount of land he owned.

Like many kings and nobles Edward owned land in more than one country. He took this for granted. When he visited his estates in south-west France where he was Duke of Gascony, he felt as much at home as he did at Westminster or Windsor.

Copy the map. (3)

1 (a) Between which years did King Edward I
(1) rule England?
(b) Why did he feel as much at home in
(3) Gascony as he did in England?
(3) (c) Why was he a good leader in wartime?
2 (a) What did a tenant have to do in return
(2) for the land he held from the king?
(b) A nobleman could be the tenant of more
(3) than one king. Look at your map to see which kings he would have paid rent to if his lands were in: (i) England, (ii) Scotland, (iii) France?
(c) Many noblemen did not feel that they belonged to one particular country. Explain
(1) why not.
3 The King of France claimed to be the
(2) overlord of Gascony.
(a) Why would it have been difficult for the king to make the duke obey him?
(b) The King of England and the King of
(3) France both wanted to control Gascony. Explain why.

▲ The lands ruled by Edward I in 1284

The growth of towns

Most of King Edward's subjects lived in villages, and made their living from farming. But there was also a growing number of towns where craftsmen such as shoemakers and silversmiths carried on their trades, and merchants made a living buying and selling goods.

By the time Edward I became King, many town merchants had become very rich. In some towns they clubbed together and bought a charter from the King giving them the right to run their towns as they pleased. Towns which had a charter from the King were known as boroughs.

On the coast of Kent and Sussex were five towns known as the Cinque Ports. These were different from other towns in England, because the King granted them special privileges. For example, their merchants were not taxed as heavily as those in other towns, and they were allowed to set up their own law courts. In return for these privileges, the merchants' ships carried supplies to the King's armies, free of charge, for fifteen days a year. The towns were Sandwich, Dover, Hythe, Romney and Hastings. By the end of the thirteenth century, Rye and Winchelsea were added to their number.

The towns were always busy. Ships docked at their quays, laden with butts of wine from Gascony and rolls of embroidered cloth from France. Wooden carts, piled high with bales of wool, clattered over the cobblestones on their way to ships anchored in the harbours, waiting to sail to Ostend or Bordeaux. It was often difficult to move in the narrow, crowded streets of the older towns, but Winchelsea was planned to allow traders to transport their goods easily to and from the harbour.

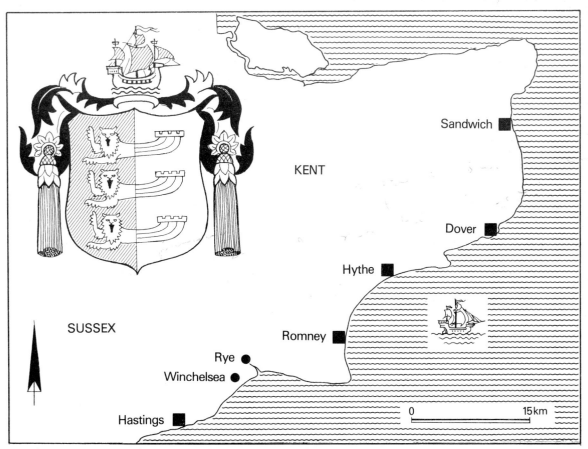

▲ The Cinque Ports. The towns had their own coat of arms, which you can see in the picture

Study

The Cinque Ports

In groups of four, make a wall display headed: The Cinque Ports.

1 Draw a picture or plan to illustrate each of these statements:
- (5) The Cinque Ports were on the English Channel.
- (5) Winchelsea was a new, well-planned town.
- (5) Merchants' families in the Cinque Ports were wealthy.
- (5) Ships from the ports carried military supplies and valuable cargoes.

2 Write one or two sentences to go with each picture.

3 Mount your work on a large piece of paper and display it.

Writing

1 By 1296 there were 730 houses in Winchelsea and 79 building plots were waiting to be developed. Describe how Adam Shipman, a trader from Hythe:
> Watched goods being loaded and unloaded at Winchelsea,
> Walked through the new town, looking at the buildings,
> Decided to build a house in Winchelsea and move there.

2 Winchelsea was governed by a mayor and twelve 'jurats' or town councillors. Write a letter that the Mayor of Winchelsea might have written in 1296 to the mayor of an inland town, explaining:
> What the duties and privileges of the Cinque Ports merchants were,
> Why he was proud to be the Mayor of Winchelsea.

3 In 1284 King Edward ordered Henry le Waleys, the Warden of the Cinque Ports, to start making plans for the new town of Winchelsea. Write the report that le Waleys might have sent to the King with the plan of Winchelsea, explaining why the new town will be
> an efficient port,
> safe from attack by land or sea.

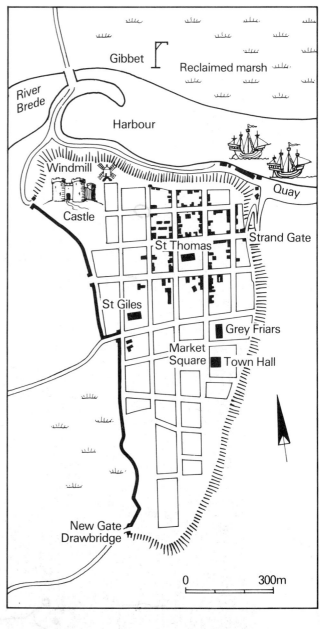

▼ Winchelsea in the fourteenth century

(Map labels: Gibbet, Reclaimed marsh, River Brede, Harbour, Windmill, Castle, St Thomas, Quay, Strand Gate, St Giles, Grey Friars, Market Square, Town Hall, New Gate Drawbridge, 0 300m)

Edward I and Parliament

Edward usually expected to get enough money from his tenants to be able to rule the country. If he needed more, he had to call a Parliament to discuss how much he needed, who should pay the extra taxes, and how the money should be collected.

Originally a Parliament was a meeting between the King and the landowners and churchmen who helped him to rule England. The name first came from the French word *parler*, meaning to talk or discuss. The King and his landowners were descended from the

▲ A sixteenth-century painting of Edward I meeting his Parliament. King Alexander of Scotland attended because he owned estates in England

9

French-speaking Normans who had conquered England in 1066, and even at the end of the thirteenth century, they still spoke French to one another.

By the end of the thirteenth century, some traders and merchants were as rich as many landowners. The King wanted to tax them as well, so after 1295 he usually summoned two representatives called *burgesses* from every large town in England to attend his Parliaments. If the King could persuade the burgesses to agree to pay a new tax, all the merchants in all the towns they represented had to pay it as well.

So in addition to obtaining men and money from his own estates, Edward was able to call on wealthy English landowners and merchants to provide him with money.

▼ A merchant and his wife

Study

Townspeople in Parliament

1 Look at the diagram opposite. Copy the sentences beneath the diagram into your (4) book, and fill in the gaps using the information given in the diagram.

2 Copy the sentence that is correct in each of these pairs of sentences:

(3)
1 for each

The King usually had to call Parliament to get enough money to run the country.
The King had to call Parliament if he needed more money than usual to run the country.

After 1295 every large town in England sent two burgesses to Parliament.
After 1295 the two largest towns in England sent burgesses to Parliament.

The King raised more money before he included the burgesses in Parliament's discussions.
The King was able to raise more money by including the burgesses in Parliament's discussions.

3 When burgesses were summoned to attend Parliament the townspeople often took the opportunity to ask the King a favour. For example, if they had built a new bridge they might ask for the right to charge the people who used it a toll. They wrote their request in a document called a petition and the (3) burgesses gave it to the King when Parliament met. Why were the townspeople sensible to ask for a favour when the King was holding a Parliament?

→

People in Parliament

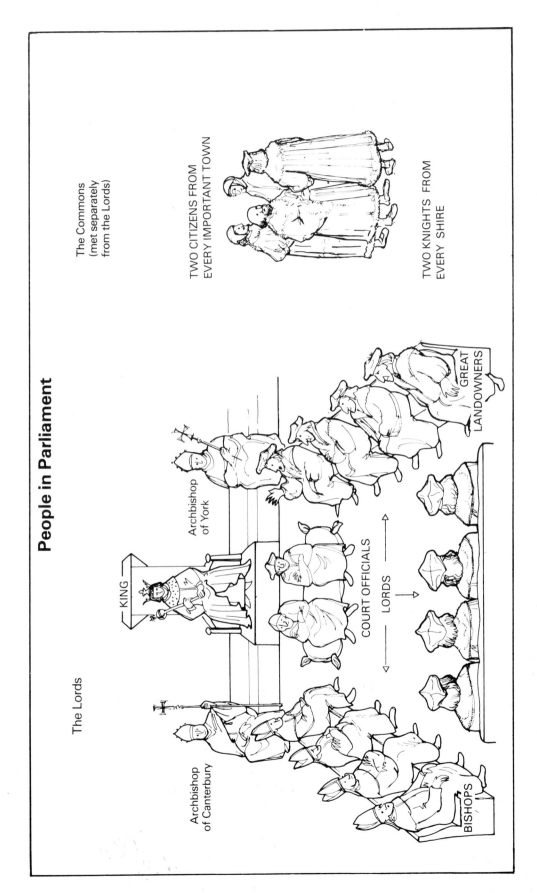

The Lords

Archbishop of Canterbury

BISHOPS

KING

Archbishop of York

COURT OFFICIALS

LORDS

GREAT LANDOWNERS

The Commons
(met separately
from the Lords)

TWO CITIZENS FROM
EVERY IMPORTANT TOWN

TWO KNIGHTS FROM
EVERY SHIRE

Look at the picture above. Using the information it gives you, copy and complete the following sentences:

In the House of Lords, the King met important churchmen, court —— and great ——.

In addition, the King summoned two —— from every shire and two —— from every town.

The Welsh wars

Edward decided to use his power and wealth to win more land for himself and his descendants. He began by invading Wales.

The war of 1276
In the middle of the thirteenth century, Wales was an independent country with its own laws and language. In 1267 Prince Llewellyn, the ruler of Wales, made a treaty with Henry III of England. He recognised Henry as his overlord, and in return Henry confirmed him as ruler of most of Wales.

When Edward I became King of England, Llewellyn refused to accept him as his overlord. He did not trust Edward. In 1276 Edward declared war on Llewellyn, and in 1277 three English armies invaded Wales. Llewellyn surrendered, and Edward took over most of his territory.

The war of 1282
After 1277 the Welsh nobles often quarrelled with the English officials who ruled the areas which Edward had conquered. The officials always wanted to use English law to try cases that came before them. The Welsh thought that Welsh laws ought to be used. In March 1282 Llewellyn's brother, David, lost patience with the English and began a revolt. Llewellyn decided to support his brother, and a full-scale war broke out between England and Wales.

Edward was not expecting a war, and had no forces ready. But in August he attacked Wales with an army of 10,000 men and a fleet of sixty ships. In November Llewellyn was killed in a skirmish, and after his death the Welsh forces were easily defeated. The revolt ended in June 1283 when David was captured. In September Edward had him tried for treason. He was found guilty and hanged.

Edward takes over
Wales was now at Edward's mercy. In March 1284 he announced that the whole country now belonged to him, and in 1301 he made his young son, Edward, Prince of Wales. King Edward appointed his own officials to govern Wales. To encourage Englishmen to settle there he built walled towns where English merchants could live in safety. He also had castles built, many of which still stand. Most were on the coast, so that if the Welsh rebelled and cut them off from the rest of the country, Edward could send men and supplies to them by sea.

Study

The castles of North Wales

Look at the map of North Wales on page 13, and find Snowdonia. This region was Llewellyn's stronghold. He and his men would ride out on a raid and then retreat to the safety of the mountains.

Now find the castles that are shown on the map. As you can see, they all stand at the foot of Snowdonia and are built on or near the coast. King Edward ordered his architects to design and build these castles. Once the work was under way, troops were stationed in them to patrol the countryside and stop the raiders leaving the mountains. The picture of Caernarfon Castle will give you some idea of how strong Edward's fortresses were. The Welsh, who saw them being built, knew how difficult it would be to capture them, and after Llewellyn and David died no other leader came forward to continue the rebellion.

Every year thousands of tourists visit the castles of North Wales. Some follow the route that Edward's army took in 1277, coming from

→ Chester along the narrow strip of land between the mountains and the coast. Others come from the south, through the Llanberis Pass, a way through the mountains that was once patrolled by Llewellyn's men. When the tourists see the rugged countryside of Snowdonia and the strong towers of Caernarfon Castle they can imagine how hard Edward and Llewellyn fought against each other for control of this region of Britain.

Make a guidebook to Caernarfon Castle

Under the heading *Croeso I Gaernarfon* (Welcome to Caernarfon), write and illustrate a guidebook to Caernarfon Castle. You might include:

(5) 1 A plan of the castle.
2 A brief account of the wars between Edward
   and Llewellyn, explaining the reasons why
(6)   Llewellyn rebelled in 1277,
(6)   David joined Llewellyn in 1284,
(4)   Edward built Caernarfon Castle.
(2) 3 Instructions on how to drive to Caernarfon.
(4) 4 Suggestions for other places in North Wales
     that a tourist interested in castles might visit.
     (5) for presentation

Library work

Look up *concentric castles* in a topic book or under the letter C in an encyclopedia.

1 Why are Edward's castles described as *concentric*?
2 How did these parts of a concentric castle help to protect its defenders? (i) the curtain wall, (ii) the flanking towers, (iii) the crenellations.

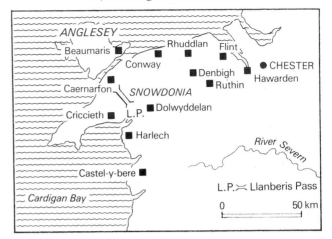

▼ North Wales, showing the castles Edward built

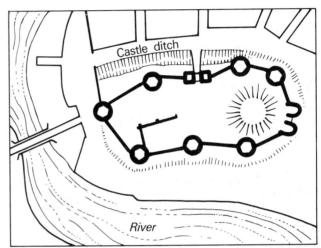

▲ Edward built Caernarfon castle on the site of a Norman motte and bailey castle

▼ Caernarfon Castle, one of the biggest and strongest castles that Edward I built in Wales. His son, Edward, was born there

The Scottish wars

The death of Alexander III

When Edward I became King of England, Scotland was ruled by Alexander III. He had married Edward's sister, and was on good terms with the English King.

One day in March 1286, Alexander was at a meeting of his Council in Edinburgh. At the end of the meeting he decided to travel to Kinghorn in Fife, where his wife was staying.

It was a cold, stormy evening as Alexander, accompanied by three attendants, galloped north from Edinburgh to the banks of the Forth at Dalmeny. The ferryman tried to persuade him to go back, but Alexander refused, and crossed to Inverkeithing.

It was now pitch dark, and Alexander asked for two local men to act as guides. As soon as they were ready the little party rode off into the night in the direction of Kinghorn. Somewhere along the way Alexander took the wrong path, and the next day he was found dead on the sea shore beneath some cliffs with his neck broken. Edward used this accident to try to take control of Scotland.

King Edward's policy

When Alexander died his granddaughter, Margaret, a little girl of three, became ruler of Scotland. In 1290 she died. She had no close relatives, and there were now thirteen people with a good claim to the throne of Scotland. The Scottish nobles feared this might lead to a civil war, and they asked Edward to choose between the claimants.

First, Edward made all the claimants agree to accept his decision. Then they had to acknowledge that as King of England he was the rightful overlord of the King of Scotland. When they had all agreed, Edward awarded the throne of Scotland to John Balliol, who probably had the best claim in any case. (See the family tree below.)

The reign of King John

Edward expected King John to obey him in everything. But the Scots thought that their king ought to have a mind of his own. John was caught between them.

In 1294 Edward declared war on King Philip of France. He ordered King John to report to him with twenty-six Scottish lords to fight against France. The Scottish nobles were very angry. They had no quarrel with King Philip, and they persuaded John to make an alliance with France against Edward. When he heard the news Edward was furious. 'Who could believe such wickedness and treachery?' he asked, and summoned his army to meet him at Newcastle-upon-Tyne. He was going to punish the Scots.

▼ This family tree shows some of the people with a claim to rule Scotland when Alexander III died in 1286

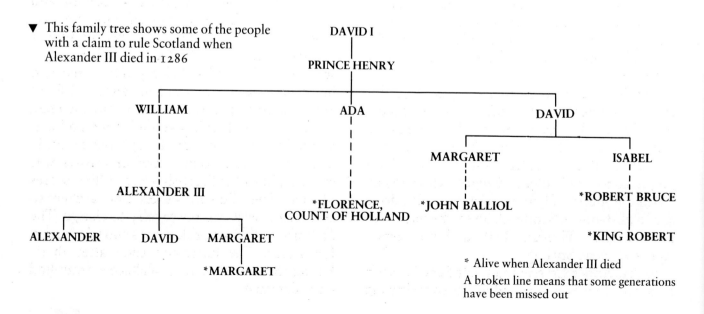

* Alive when Alexander III died

A broken line means that some generations have been missed out

14

The defeat of King John

In March 1296 Edward and his army moved north to Berwick. They smashed the wooden defences and entered the town. Edward decided to make an example of Berwick, which was the largest town in Scotland. So his troops murdered, burnt and looted, and by the time Edward left, the town was a blackened ruin.

From Berwick the English moved relentlessly north. At Dunbar their army defeated the Scots under King John, and in July John himself surrendered. Edward sent him to England where he was held captive for a few years. Then he was released and went to France. He spent the rest of his life on his family's estates there.

Edward takes over in Scotland

Most Scots took it for granted that Edward would appoint a new King of Scotland, but he decided to do the same as he had in Wales and rule the country himself. He took the Stone of Scone on which Scottish kings sat at their coronations and sent it to Westminster Abbey in London. When he left Scotland, he put Hugh Cressingham, one of his judges, in charge of the country.

One of Cressingham's jobs was to supervise the rebuilding of Berwick, which Edward intended to be the new capital of Scotland. Architects and skilled masons came from towns all over England to Berwick, where they built a new town, protected by strong stone walls.

Wallace's rebellion

King Edward left Scotland at the end of 1296. He found he needed men and money to go to war against France, and he decided to make the Scots pay higher taxes and supply men to fight in his army.

The Scots were used to having to fight for their own kings, but they had never asked them to travel further than the north of England. Edward expected them to fight in France and Flanders. They decided not to go. They preferred to join William Wallace, who had just killed the Sheriff of Lanark, and wanted to drive the English out of Scotland. So by the middle of the summer Wallace had a large army, stationed near Stirling.

In September Cressingham left Berwick with an army of 10,000 men and marched to Stirling

▼ The Stone of Scone is still in Westminster Abbey. It is part of the Coronation Chair, on which all British monarchs sit when they are crowned

to attack Wallace. But he was defeated by the Scottish army. Many English knights, including Cressingham himself, were killed. When the Scots found Cressingham's body they carefully skinned it, dried the skin, cut it into small pieces and distributed them as souvenirs.

In 1298 Edward returned to Britain and advanced into Scotland to deal with Wallace. The English forces found the Scottish army near Falkirk. Most of Wallace's soldiers were spearsmen. Edward had plenty of bowmen, and he ordered them to stay at a distance and shoot at the Scottish spearsmen. All the bowmen had to do was stand still, take their time and aim carefully, knowing that the spearsmen could not touch them. Soon a hail of arrows was thudding into the Scottish army, killing scores of men. Then Edward ordered his archers to stop firing, and told his cavalry to charge. The Scottish spearsmen broke ranks and tried to run for safety. The horsemen rode after them, killing them as they ran. Wallace's army had been defeated.

The death of Wallace

Wallace escaped after the battle at Falkirk, but in 1305 he was captured and taken to London. On 23 August, in Westminster Hall, he was tried for treason and murder. He was found guilty, and was sentenced to be tied to a hurdle and dragged for four miles through the streets of London to Smithfield. There he was to be hanged, cut down while he was still alive, disembowelled and cut into quarters. Edward devised this horrible punishment specially for Wallace. It was to become the usual punishment for traitors.

The sentence was carried out. Afterwards Wallace's head was put on display on London Bridge, and the four quarters of his body were hung up in Newcastle, Berwick, Stirling and Perth.

Study

Use your imagination

1 Jean Ferguson is married to Hamish, the ferryman at Dalmeny. She and her family live in a hut on the banks of the Firth of Forth. Describe how she is one of the last people to see King Alexander alive.
Things to write about:
King Alexander and his attendants arrive at the hut.
Jean watches her husband and son set out to ferry the King across the rough waters of the Forth.
She spends a sleepless night, hoping they are safe.
Late next day, her husband and son return with the news that the King is dead.
(Think of a time when you waited anxiously for someone to come home safely.)

2 David Roberts is an innkeeper in the new town of Berwick. It is nine years since his son Jamie disappeared, on the night when the English burnt down the old town. One day in 1305 his son comes to the inn. Write what Jamie might have said to his father to explain why he had stayed away so long, and why he had now returned to Berwick.
Things to write about:
Jamie decides to fight against the English when they burn down Berwick in 1296.
He joins Wallace's army and fights at Stirling and Falkirk.
He goes into hiding as Wallace is captured.
In 1305 he hears that Wallace is dead and goes to Berwick to see if the news is true.

(Think of a time when you risked getting into trouble by standing up for what you thought was right but tried not to involve other people.)

3 Earl Ranulf is pleased when his son, Hugo, who will inherit his lands, is born in 1290. Ranulf is a tenant of the King of Scotland. As well as his Scottish estates he has land in England and Normandy, so he is also a tenant of the King of England. He knows that each King has the right to ask for his help in wartime and to confiscate his land if he refuses. The time chart below shows you how Ranulf behaved towards the Kings of Scotland and England between 1290 and 1297.

1290	Pledged his loyalty to Edward of England as Scotland's overlord.
1294	Urged King John of Scotland to ally with Philip of France against Edward.
1296	Pledged his loyalty to Edward again when John was defeated at Dunbar.
1297	Joined the rebellion against Edward.

Write what Ranulf might have said in answer to this question: 'You pledged your loyalty to King Edward twice and each time you broke your promise. How can you justify your actions?'

16

Scotland wins her freedom

The rise of Robert Bruce

When Wallace was defeated Scotland was left without a leader. But soon a new one came forward. His name was Robert Bruce.

Bruce was a rich and powerful landowner who had a good claim to the Scottish throne. In 1304 his father died, and Robert inherited all his estates. In Scotland most of his land was in Galloway, but he also owned some land in the north-east. In England he held large estates in Hertfordshire, the manor of Tottenham in Middlesex, and a house in London. But all this was not enough. Robert was determined to become King of Scotland.

The murder of 'Red Comyn'

Robert knew that to become King he needed the help of other Scottish nobles. The most important was John Comyn, nicknamed 'Red Comyn', Lord of Badenoch. He had huge estates and powerful friends in the north-east of Scotland. If Bruce had Comyn on his side, he was bound to succeed. So in February 1306 he arranged to meet Comyn for a conference in the church of Greyfriars at Dumfries.

Nobody knows what the two men said to each other at this conference. At first they seemed to be friendly. But soon they began to quarrel. Bruce lost his temper, drew a dagger, stabbed Comyn and left him dead on the church floor.

The coronation of Bruce

At the end of March, a few weeks after the murder, Robert Bruce went to Scone, and was crowned King of Scotland. But this did not mean that he was in control of the country. Comyn's friends wanted revenge for his death, and Bruce had to defeat them before he could be accepted as King. He also had to reckon with Edward I, King of England.

The defeat of Robert Bruce

When he heard that Bruce had been crowned, Edward ordered his lieutenant in Scotland, Aymer de Valence, Comyn's brother-in-law, to find Bruce and his friends, burn, slay and 'raise dragon'. So Valence's men fought with a dragon banner at their head. This warned that they would kill all their prisoners.

Valence's army attacked Bruce at Methven near Perth on 19 June. Bruce was defeated, and fled to Ireland. While he was away Edward divided up his estates and gave them away. His family and friends were arrested. Many were hanged, including the Earl of Atholl, who was related to Edward. Someone pointed this out, thinking that Edward might spare his life. All he said was, 'In that case let him be hanged from a higher gallows than anyone else.'

Some of Bruce's supporters were imprisoned. His sister Mary and the Countess of Buchan were both held in specially made cages in castle towers at Roxburgh and Berwick.

The return of Bruce

The rebellion seemed to be over. But in 1307 Bruce returned to Scotland. He knew that Edward was old and ill, and in fact the King of England died at Burgh on Sands in Cumbria in July 1307. His death was a great help to Robert,

▲ This statue of King Robert stands on the site of the battle of Bannockburn. It was erected in 1964, the 650th anniversary of the battle

17

because the new King of England, Edward II, was not really interested in war and politics. He preferred to stay at home, give parties for his friends and write poetry.

Robert's army

Robert also knew that he had a good army. His soldiers were tough and experienced. A French writer described how they used to ride over the hill passes on their hardy mountain ponies. Every man carried all that he needed—a shield and a spear, a bag of oatmeal and a thick metal plate. If they wanted meat they killed a cow and boiled pieces of it in a bag made of its own skin. For most of the time they lived on oatmeal, which they made into cakes. They mixed the meal into a paste with water and cooked it on their metal plates over a fire.

Most armies moved very slowly because they needed heavy wagons to carry tents, pots, pans and all the rest of their equipment. Bruce's army had no wagons, so they could move quickly— up to 40 kilometres in a day. They could gallop through the night, take their enemies by surprise and defeat them before they had time to prepare for battle.

Capturing castles

Bruce's army also used surprise tactics to capture castles. At Perth they waded silently through the moat at dead of night with water up to their necks. They carried long, light ladders, and when they reached the other side of the moat they hooked the ladders onto the castle wall and scrambled up.

At Edinburgh a small group of men made a noisy attack on one part of the wall. As all the defenders ran to drive them off, a much larger party silently climbed the steep crags on the other side and got over the wall unopposed.

At Linlithgow a farmer delivering a load of hay to the castle jammed his cart in the entrance so that the doors would not shut, and the portcullis stuck halfway down. Then Bruce's men, who had been hiding nearby, ran forward and forced their way into the castle.

By the summer of 1314 the Scots had driven the English out of most of the castles in the Scottish lowlands. But the English still held Stirling. Edward Bruce, Robert's brother, had been besieging it for months, but it was a very strong fortress, and he did not dare attack it. In June 1313 he had made a truce with the castle governor, Sir Philip Moubray, who had agreed to hand over the castle if no army came to relieve it by midsummer 1314.

The battle of Bannockburn, 1314

Edward II had to try to save Stirling. So in spring 1314 he collected a large army and advanced into Scotland.

At midsummer the English army camped near Stirling on the banks of a stream called the Bannock burn. There was only a small area of dry ground, surrounded by water and marsh. Bruce realised that the English army had no room to spread out in battle formation. So he ordered his troops to attack.

The Scots won a great victory. The English troops were too close together and their longbowmen had no room to form up and take proper aim. Edward and his army were defeated. Edward managed to escape, but many of his troops were trapped in the Bannock burn and died in the muddy water. It was eight years before Edward invaded Scotland again.

In the meantime Bruce did everything he could to try to force Edward to make peace. Every year Scottish armies rode into the north of England capturing castles, destroying towns and burning crops. But this had little effect on Edward, who spent most of his time in the south of the country.

The Declaration of Arbroath

The Scots also tried to get support from overseas. In 1320 about forty Scottish nobles sent a letter from Arbroath to the Pope, who supported the English side. In this letter they

▲ A photograph of the Declaration of Arbroath. The seals hanging from it are those of the Scottish nobles who sent it to the Pope

explained why they supported King Robert against Edward. 'We will,' they said, 'never on any conditions be subjected to the leadership of the English. For we fight not for glory, nor riches, nor honours, but for freedom alone, which no man gives up except with his life.'

The end of the war

The war dragged on for several more years. In 1323 the two countries agreed on a truce for 13 years. But in 1327 Edward II was murdered. His son, Edward III, needed peace with Scotland. So in 1328 he signed the Treaty of Northampton, which declared Scotland to be a free and independent country. Though war broke out again in 1333, and continued off and on for more than 200 years, the Kings of England never again claimed the right to rule Scotland. The two kingdoms were united in 1603, when James VI of Scotland became King James I of England as well.

▼ The vicars of Corbridge in Northumberland lived in this tower next to the church. These fortified towers, known as peels, were built to protect the inhabitants from Scottish raiding parties

Study

Bruce and his enemies

1 (a) Copy the time chart opposite and fill in the blank spaces.
(b) Give your time chart a title.
(c) For how many years did Robert Bruce fight the English?

2 (a) Why did Aymer de Valence help Edward to fight Robert Bruce?
(b) How did Aymer de Valence behave towards his enemies when he 'raised dragon'?
(c) Give an example of Edward's harsh treatment of Bruce's followers.

3 (a) Why did Bruce's men not need slow, heavy wagons to transport
     (i) cooking pots, (ii) seige engines?
(b) What advantage did their methods of fighting give them over the English?
(c) What difficulties defeated Edward II when he invaded Scotland in 1322?

Date	Important event
____	Bruce inherits lands in England and Scotland.
1306	Bruce rebels against _____, kills _____ and declares himself King of Scotland. Later, he is forced to flee to Ireland.
____	Edward I dies. Bruce returns to Scotland and fights the English.
1314	Battle of _____. The Scots drive the English from Scotland.
____	Edward II invades Scotland. He is defeated.
1328	Treaty of _____. Scotland is declared independent.

The Hundred Years War

War breaks out

The period from 1337 to 1453 is often called the Hundred Years War because England and France were fighting each other for most of the time. The quarrel began over Gascony, a rich wine-growing area in the south-west of France.

The Kings of England had been Dukes of Gascony ever since the middle of the twelfth century. The duchy paid taxes to the King, and there was a flourishing trade between the two countries. English merchants imported wine from Gascony, and exported English wheat.

The Kings of England took it for granted that they were the rightful owners of Gascony. The French Kings disagreed. They believed that Gascony was French, and thought it ought to belong to them. Neither side would give way, and there were frequent quarrels between them.

The situation got worse in 1334. England and Scotland were at war, and Philip VI welcomed King David of Scotland to France. In revenge Edward III of England gave shelter to Robert of Artois, an enemy of King Philip. This made Philip so angry that he said he would occupy Gascony. Edward then declared that he, not Philip, was the rightful King of France, and in 1337 he declared war.

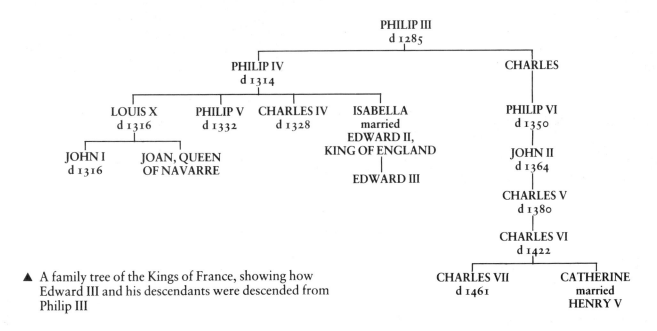

▲ A family tree of the Kings of France, showing how Edward III and his descendants were descended from Philip III

Sluys and Crécy

The battle of Sluys, 1340

In 1340 Philip VI was preparing to invade England. At Sluys in Flanders he had a great fleet of ships ready to carry his army across the Channel. Edward III decided to prevent the invasion by attacking the French fleet. He had no navy, so he forced merchants and fishermen to lend him ships. He packed the boats with archers and men-at-arms and sailed across to Sluys.

At 5 a.m. on 24 June the English ships, with the wind, the tide and the rising sun behind them, swept down on the French fleet. Philip was expecting an attack. He had chained his boats together to form three huge floating platforms, and had put 20,000 men on board to defend them.

As the English ships came within bowshot their archers began to shoot at the French. Then the ships rammed into the French boats. The English men-at-arms jumped onto them and attacked the soldiers and sailors with swords, axes and spears. Very few of the French had been properly trained. Many were killed and the rest fled, jumping from boat to boat to escape. By the end of the day the whole of the French fleet had either been sunk or captured. The danger of invasion was over.

The battle of Crécy, 1346

For the rest of the war most of the fighting took place in France. Occasionally French troops invaded Gascony. It was difficult for the English to send an army all the way to south-west France to drive them out, so as a rule the English landed in the north of France and laid waste the countryside to force the French to bring troops back from Gascony to defend it.

For example, in 1346 the French invaded Gascony and Edward III landed on the north coast of France with an army of 15,000 men. They plundered the towns of Cherbourg and Caen, and advanced towards Paris. On their way they killed the peasants and their animals, burnt houses, mills, crops and haystacks, and captured landowners to hold to ransom. Within a few weeks they had reached Poissy, only 30 kilometres from Paris.

Philip quickly got together a large army consisting mostly of knights on horseback and advanced on the English. Edward retreated to Crécy, about 80 kilometres south of Calais. He drew up his army along the top of a ridge. His men-at-arms were in the centre. His long-bowmen were drawn up on each side of them at

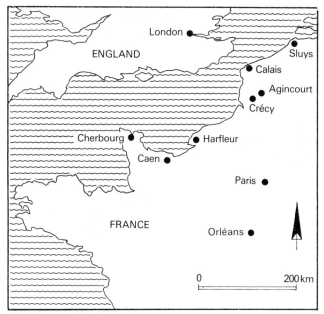

▲ Northern France

an angle to the ridge so that they could shoot at the flanks of the advancing enemy.

The French army came into sight in the early evening of 26 August. Many of Philip's knights were landowners who had come from their estates to fight for the King. Though they had taken part in tournaments, many of them had never fought in a battle before. Philip realised that the English army was in a very strong position, and decided not to attack until the next day. But before he could tell his knights, they were riding up the hill towards the English.

► A fourteenth-century drawing of bowmen practising. Longbows varied in size. Usually their length was about the same as the height of the bowman. So a man 2 metres tall used a bow 2 metres long

Italian crossbowmen ran along in front of them. Their job was to kill or injure as many of the enemy as possible before the knights charged in to finish them off.

As the crossbowmen ran up the hill the English longbowmen waited with their bows and arrows at the ready. Then Edward gave them a signal and they shot volleys of arrows at the Italians. One onlooker said that there were so many arrows in the air that it looked as if it was snowing. The crossbowmen stopped in their tracks. The galloping French knights rode over them, but they too were stopped by the arrows of the English bowmen and forced to retreat.

The French knights charged fifteen times, but were always driven back. By the time the battle ended it was dark. The next day the English counted the dead, and discovered that more than 12,000 of the French army had been killed.

Edward's army had won a great victory. He then went on to capture the port of Calais, which the English kept right through the war. In 1347 Edward and Philip made a truce, and the English army sailed back to England.

Poitiers and Agincourt

Poitiers and Charles V

The truce did not last. In 1356 Edward III's son, the Black Prince, captured the French King, John II, in a battle at Poitiers and brought him back to England. The French paid a ransom of 3 million gold crowns to get him back and the war dragged on.

In 1364 King John died. His son, Charles V, used new methods to try to defeat the English. Instead of leading a large army against the invaders he sent small bands of men to attack supply wagons and isolated outposts. This wore the English down, and in 1396 Richard II, the Black Prince's son, signed a peace treaty.

The battle of Agincourt, 1415

Richard and Henry IV who followed him as King both had to deal with rebellions in England, and could not spare the time or the money to fight overseas. But when Henry V became King in 1413 he decided to invade France. The French King, Charles VI, was mad, and Henry thought it would be easy to defeat him and become King of France himself.

In the middle of August 1415 Henry landed with an army of 10,000 men on the French coast near the port of Harfleur. The town was defended by a strong stone wall with 26 towers. The citizens refused to surrender, so Henry surrounded it, and began to destroy its defences.

Before about 1350 there was no quick, sure way to overcome strong stone walls. At the beginning of the fourteenth century engineers in Europe had invented cannons which used gunpowder to fire arrows, stones and bullets. At first these cannons were small and unreliable, but gradually they improved and by

▲ The sculptor of this statue of Charles V took care to make it a good likeness. Most medieval pictures and statues of kings do not look much like them. Instead they show how the artist thought a king should look

▼ A fifteenth-century drawing of a town under siege. Some of the attackers have small guns, but most carry bows and arrows. On the left are two cannons protected by a thick wooden shield

1415 Henry had iron guns 3 metres long, which fired stone balls 60 centimetres in diameter, weighing nearly half a tonne.

Henry used his cannons to batter Harfleur, and by the middle of September he had destroyed several sections of the wall. On 22 September the inhabitants surrendered, so Henry left a small garrison there and moved further into France with the rest of his army.

Henry had intended to attack Paris, but many of his men had fallen ill during the siege of Harfleur, and a number had died. Now he had only 7,000 men. It was too few to launch an attack on Paris. Instead Henry decided to march north to Calais, and return to England.

As he set off with his men, it began to rain. Food was short, and there was little shelter. More of his men fell ill, and by the time he reached the village of Agincourt 60 kilometres south of Calais, he had only 6,000 left.

At Agincourt Henry found his way blocked by an army of more than 40,000 men. He offered to give up Harfleur and pay for all the damage his army had done if the French would let him through to Calais. But they refused, so Henry had to fight.

The next day he ordered his bowmen to advance to about 300 metres from the French. Each man carried a pointed stake which he hammered into the ground, pointing towards the enemy. Then the bowmen began to shoot.

The French knights thought it would be easy to drive the archers away. So they charged them. It was a great mistake. The ground was very muddy after the rain. This slowed down the horses carrying knights in heavy armour. They made an easy target for the bowmen. The knights who reached the English lines were stopped by the sharpened stakes pointing at their horses' chests. As they slowed down, lightly armed men dashed out from behind the English lines, pulled the knights from their horses and stabbed them to death through the joints in their armour.

The French charged twice, but failed to break through. In all about 10,000 of them were killed. After the second charge they did not dare try again. Instead they retreated, leaving the road to Calais open for Henry and his troops.

The French admit defeat

Henry V won a great victory at Agincourt. He returned to England for the winter, but the next year he led another army to France. He conquered most of Normandy, and the French decided that they must make peace. So they signed a treaty allowing Henry to marry Charles VI's daughter, Catherine, and giving him the right to become King of France when Charles died. It seemed that England had won the war.

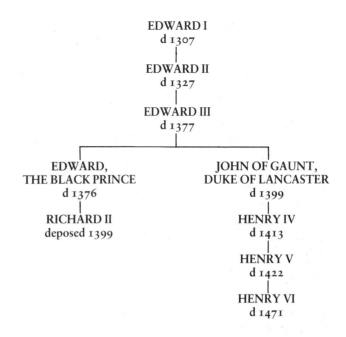

▲ Kings of England, 1307–1471

The French fight back

Joan of Arc

As it turned out, Henry died before Charles, leaving a baby son to succeed him. The French took heart and slowly began to drive the English out of Normandy. They were encouraged by Joan of Arc, a peasant girl who claimed that she could hear the voices of Christ and his saints. The voices ordered her to crown Charles, the old king's son, King of France, and drive the English out.

In the Middle Ages most people believed that anyone claiming to hear such voices was in touch with either God or the Devil. The French believed that Joan's voices came from God. The English said that she was a witch, and that it was the Devil's voice that she heard.

The French put Joan in charge of their army. She was certain that she could defeat the English, and was not afraid to lead troops into battle herself. In May 1429 she attacked an English army which was besieging the town of Orléans, and drove them away. In June her troops defeated another English army at Patay, and in July she crowned Charles VII King of France in Rheims Cathedral. But then the English captured her. She refused to admit that

her voices might come from the Devil, so they put her on trial for heresy and burnt her at the stake.

The defeat of the English

After Joan's death Charles VII took charge. France was a rich country, and Charles made his people pay heavy taxes. He used the money to train and equip a full-time army. He also employed a chemist and cannon maker named John Bureau. Bureau invented a mill which ground gunpowder into finer particles than before. This made it explode with greater force. He also designed new guns, some of which were so light that a man could carry them about and fire them on his own.

With their new equipment the French steadily drove the English out of Normandy and Gascony. By 1453 the town of Calais was the only part of France still ruled by the English, and the two sides made peace at last.

In the Hundred Years War the Kings of England lost Gascony, which they had ruled for 300 years. In 1558 the French captured Calais, and the Kings of England were left with England, Wales and the Channel Islands.

Study

The Lions and the Lilies

The standards

When the armies of the King of England and the King of France went to war, a standard-bearer on each side carried his King's standard into battle. During the battle, the troops could tell where their commander was by looking for the standard, and men who were separated from their comrades in the confusion of the fighting could use it as a rallying point.

The emblem on each standard was bold and clear so that it could not be mistaken for the enemy's, and while the soldiers could see it flying over the field they knew that they still had a chance of victory.

The English standard

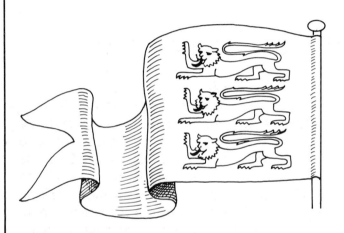

The French standard

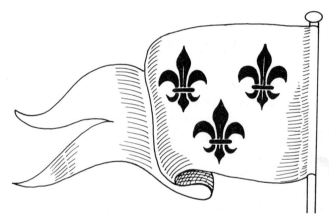

The battles of the Hundred Years War

1 (a) Taking a whole page in your book, copy the table on page 27 and fill in the gaps in the first four columns.

(b) Fill in the column headed 'King's emblem' by drawing either a lion or a lily (look at the standards above) to show the emblem of the winning side.

(c) Name (i) the event in 1429 that marked the first great French victory against the English, (ii) the Frenchwoman who was responsible for this success.

2 (a) Draw the picture of longbowmen on page 22.

(b) Give an example to show how the English used bowmen at sea in the Hundred Years War.

(c) Name two battles in which English bowmen were able to hold off an attack by French knights.

3 (a) Copy the map of France on page 22.

(b) Why (i) was Gascony valuable to the Kings of England, (ii) was Charles VII able to drive the English out of Gascony and defeat the English?

(c) Which French port did the English capture in 1346 and hold until 1558?

→

The battles of the Hundred Years War

Date	Battle	Land or sea	Victor	King's emblem
1340	Sluys		Edward III	
	Crécy		Edward III	
1346		Land		
1347	Truce between Edward III and King Philip of France			
	Agincourt	Land		
	Peace Treaty	Henry V married Catherine of France		
1429	Siege of Orléans	Land		
1453	Peace Treaty, after French victories. The English give up all their possessions in France except the town of Calais			

The effects of the Hundred Years War

The cost of the war

In the eleventh century wars had been cheap. The army had consisted of part-time, unpaid soldiers who left their land for a few months to fight for the King and then returned home. But the defeat of the French knights at Crécy and Agincourt showed that in the fourteenth century this system no longer worked. To fight a successful campaign a king needed a professional army of trained soldiers who obeyed orders instantly and had learnt how to use their weapons properly.

The King had to pay these men to fight. This was very expensive. At a time when a ploughman was paid 2 pence a day a knight in full armour expected 2 shillings, and a bowman 3 pence. The new cannons were also expensive. So the King was forced to tax the people to pay for the war. In 1340 Edward III demanded a ninth of everybody's movable property—a ninth of the farmer's crops and animals, and a ninth of the merchant's money and stock. By 1377 the treasury was empty again, and Parliament demanded a new tax of 4 pence a head which everybody had to pay. These taxes were very unpopular and eventually led to a rebellion.

The profits of war

Some people in Britain benefited from the war. Soldiers who fought in France took everything of value they could carry from the towns and villages they conquered. At the end of the campaign they took their booty back to England and, according to a chronicler writing in the middle of the fourteenth century, 'there were few women who did not possess something from Caen, Calais or another town over the seas, such as clothing, furs and cushions'.

A few men made fortunes. Before 1415 young John Fastolf of Caister, in Norfolk, owned enough land to bring him an income of £46 a year. Then he fought at Agincourt with Henry V and went on several more campaigns in France. When he died in 1459 he had an income of £1,450 a year, and had built himself a castle at Caister, part of which still stands.

The language of the people

At the beginning of the fourteenth century the King of England and his courtiers still spoke French. But as the wars against France dragged on, they began to speak English, using the dialect spoken by people living in and around

▼ Bodiam Castle, in Sussex, was built by Sir Edward Dallingridge at the end of the fourteenth century. He paid for it with money he had made fighting in France with the Black Prince

London. This dialect became known as the King's English.

The first person to write great stories in the King's English was Geoffrey Chaucer, a government official. He called his book *The Canterbury Tales*. It describes how, one April, the author went to the Tabard Inn, just outside London. The inn was crowded with pilgrims meeting there before riding to Canterbury to pray at the shrine of St Thomas Becket.

According to the book, the author decided to go with them. Before they set out the landlord of the inn suggested that, to pass the time on the journey, each pilgrim should tell the others two stories on the way to Canterbury, and two on the way back. The pilgrims thought this was a good idea, and agreed that when they got back to the Tabard they would club together and buy supper for the person who had told the best story.

The pilgrims came from all over England. There were monks and nuns, scholars and lawyers, townspeople, workers on the land, and a knight and his son who had just returned from the wars overseas. They told all kinds of stories. Some were very funny, and all Chaucer's readers were able to find something in *The Canterbury Tales* to interest them and make them laugh.

Chaucer's stories helped to spread the King's English to other parts of England where people spoke different dialects.

Study

The pilgrims ride to Canterbury

The Serjeant at Law

The Knight

The Wife of Bath

Group work

In groups of three:

1 Choose one picture each of the pilgrims.
2 Draw your picture and colour it. In the manuscript from which the pictures are taken, the pilgrims' clothes are coloured as follows:

> Serjeant at Law: robes—scarlet; trimmings—blue; hood—white.
> Wife of Bath: gown—red; foot-mantle or leggings—blue.
> Knight: head-covering—dark brown; coat—dark blue; spurs—gold.

3 One of the sentences below will fit the character that you have drawn. Choose the correct one and copy it under your drawing:

> A good wif was ther of beside Bath.
> Justice he was ful often in assize.
> He was a verray parfit, gentil knight.

4 Cut round your picture and the writing under it and mount it on a large sheet of plain paper. Draw a background showing the Tabard Inn, some houses and a sign saying *To Canterbury*.
5 Display your work.

Further work

Writing

1 (a) Write a list of three or more reasons why the Scots admired Robert Bruce.
 (b) Write a paragraph under the heading: 'Robert Bruce—a Scottish hero', turning your list into interesting sentences.
2 (a) Make a list of three or more reasons why some French people thought that Joan of Arc was a saint, while others thought that she was doing the Devil's work.
 (b) Write a paragraph under the heading: 'Joan of Arc—Saint or Witch?' turning your list into interesting sentences.
3 (a) Make a list of three or more examples to show that Edward I was a firm leader.
 (b) Make a list of reasons why the Scots thought that Edward I was a tyrant.
 (c) Write two paragraphs under the title: 'King Edward I of England', turning your lists into interesting sentences.

Drawing

1 (a) Draw the family tree of the Kings of England on page 25.

(b) Look carefully at the family tree and write a sentence explaining why the Black Prince never became King of England.

(c) Look at the family tree of the Kings of France on page 21. Which King of France was an ancestor of both the Black Prince and Charles V of France?

2 (a) Draw three or four pictures to illustrate the section headed 'Capturing castles' on page 18. For example, you might draw a picture of men carrying ladders to put against a castle wall.

(b) Write a sentence under each of your pictures, explaining what it shows.

(c) Compare the picture that you have drawn with the picture of a town under siege on page 24. What weapons were being used to attack castles in France in the fifteenth century that were not invented when Bruce's men were attacking castles in Scotland in the fourteenth century?

3 (a) Many artists have drawn pictures of Joan of Arc, showing their idea of what she looked like. A knight who knew Joan said that the first time he saw her, she was dressed in 'poor woman's clothing' of a reddish-brown colour. Another knight said that when Joan set out with the soldiers to fight, she 'put on a man's tunic and clothes, hose, leggings, sword and the like'. We also know that she had dark hair. Draw a picture of Joan of Arc as *you* imagine her, showing her dressed *either* as a poor peasant girl *or* as a soldier.

(b) Whose voices did Joan say had told her to drive the English out of France?

Drama

In groups of three:

1 Read the description of the battle of Agincourt starting on page 23.

2 Below are the beginnings of two scenes for a play about the battle of Agincourt, showing 3 English bowmen before and after the battle. Taking one character each, complete both scenes, giving each bowman at least two more things to say.

3 Learn your words.

4 Choose three groups to perform their scenes to the class.

Scene 1

It is evening. A steady drizzle of rain is falling. Three English bowmen are huddled over a smoky fire. They look cold and hungry.

STEPHEN: This rain is making my bones ache.

GILES: How I'll have the strength to bend a bow tomorrow I don't know.

THOMAS: Stop complaining, you two. I've got enough to put up with.

Scene 2

It is late afternoon the next day. The rain has stopped and the sun is coming out from behind the clouds. The three men have returned to their camp-site.

THOMAS: What a victory! I never thought I'd live to see the end of this day.

GILES: Neither did I when I saw those French knights riding.

STEPHEN: Is that blood on your tunic, Thomas?

Quiz

1 *True or false?*

A barrel of salted fish was called a *burgess*.

The Scots skinned an Englishman after the Battle of Stirling Bridge.

By the end of the Hundred Years War, Paris was the only town in France that was still ruled by the English.

2 Make up your own 'True or false?' questions and write them on separate pieces of paper. Give them in and hold your quiz.

Glossary

Add these words to your glossary and explain what each of them means:

negotiations   treaty   conference   heresy

Library work

Look up Guilds or Gilds under the letter G in an encyclopedia or in the Index of a book on the Middle Ages.

1 What was a guild?

2 What can you find out about these people?

apprentices   journeymen   masters

2 The Black Death and the Peasants' Revolt

The men of Fobbing

The poll tax

Fobbing was a small village on the coast of Essex. Its people worked hard. Most of the men were farm labourers but some had boats and went fishing, and a few, like the baker and the carpenter, were tradesmen.

In 1381 the villagers were angry. They thought they were paying too many taxes. In addition to taxes on their land and possessions they all had to pay a new poll tax whether they owned any property or not.

The first time Parliament approved a poll tax in 1377 it was only a groat (4 pence) a head. The villagers grumbled, but they paid. So did everyone else. But in 1381 Parliament voted three groats a head. The government needed the money to fight the war against France.

Many people thought the new tax was too high and refused to pay. So when the treasurer worked out how much the tax had brought in, he found it was much less than he had expected. He decided to send out special commissioners to make the people pay.

John Bampton goes to Brentwood

In Essex the commissioner was John Bampton, a local landowner, and one day at the end of May the men of Fobbing and nearby villages were ordered to go to Brentwood to meet him.

Bampton told the villagers that he knew that many of them had not paid their poll tax. Every village would have to pay more. He turned to the men of Fobbing and began to work out how much extra they would have to pay.

The villagers defy Bampton

The men of Fobbing were very angry. One of them, Thomas the Baker, spoke up. He told Bampton that they had a certificate from the tax collector saying that they had paid their share of the poll tax, so they had decided not to hand over any more.

Bampton told the men not to be stupid. He had two armed guards with him, and he warned everyone that these men-at-arms would arrest all those who refused to pay their share of the extra tax.

The villagers left the courtroom. That evening they talked to men from Corringham and Stanford, the two villages nearest to Fobbing, and they all agreed that, whatever happened, they were not going to pay any more money.

They chase Bampton away

The next day a hundred men went back to court and told Bampton what they had decided. He was very angry, and ordered his men to arrest them all. But there were too many villagers. Shouting and cheering, they took his men's weapons and drove Bampton and his soldiers out of the courtroom and along the road. Bampton locked himself in his lodgings and then, in the evening when all was quiet, he mounted his horse and rode off to London to report to the King's Council.

Meanwhile the Essex villagers set off for home. They were not sorry for what they had done, for they hated tax collectors, but when

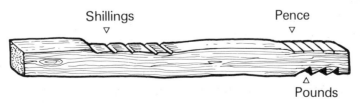

▲ A tax tally. When a man paid taxes into the treasury, an official recorded the amount by cutting notches on a piece of hazel wood. Then he split the wood down the middle, and handed over one half as a receipt

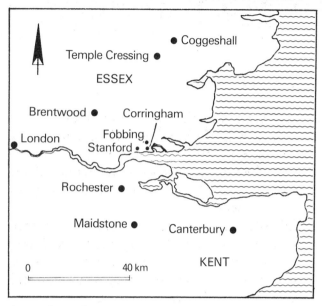

accused them. Then the men of Fobbing let him go and he returned to London.

The revolt spreads

Some of the men were not satisfied. They wanted revenge on the jurors who had informed against them. They tracked three of them down, dragged them out of their houses, beheaded them and then set fire to the houses. They also captured and beheaded three clerks who had worked for John Bampton.

The villagers were now in even greater danger. They had threatened one of the King's judges and murdered six innocent men, three of them government officials. They could expect no mercy from the King's Council. So they went from village to village, asking men to join them in a march on London to force the King to dismiss his advisers and take more notice of the wishes of ordinary people.

Wherever they went in Essex and Kent they found plenty of men willing to join them. Soon they had a huge army ready to march on London. A great revolt had begun.

they thought over what had happened they were very frightened. They knew that the Council would try to punish them for defying and chasing away the King's commissioner. So instead of going home they hid in the woods nearby where they thought they would be safe.

The chief justice arrives

Sure enough, a few days later the Council sent the chief justice, Sir Robert Belknap, to find out who had attacked Bampton and to put them on trial. Sir Robert called a jury of 12 men from the district and asked them who the guilty men were. Soon he had a list of names.

When the men of Fobbing heard what was going on they became angry and desperate. They hated lawyers and judges because they always seemed to be on the side of the rich who could afford to pay their fees. In addition, they knew that if they were put on trial they would probably be hanged.

The chief justice leaves

By chance the villagers heard that Sir Robert had only two men-at-arms with him. So they decided to frighten him off. A great crowd of men armed with clubs and axes went to see the judge. They told him that unless he returned to London at once and promised never to come back, they would certainly kill him.

Sir Robert could see that they were in earnest. He swore on the Bible not to make any more inquiries. He also named the jurors who had

▲ In the later Middle Ages, the tombs of rich men and women were decorated with their portraits engraved on sheets of brass. This one, made in 1440, shows Thomas Rolfe, a lawyer from Gosfield in Essex

Studying the story

How do we know?

The 'Anonymous Chronicle'

The story that you have just read comes from a chronicle called the 'Anonymous Chronicle'. It was given this name because we do not know who wrote it. As far as we can tell, its author was a monk who lived in York at the end of the fourteenth century. Some parts of his chronicle sound like an eye-witness account but we do not know if he saw what happened himself, or copied something he read in another chronicle. When we know so little about an author and where his information came from we have to test his story carefully to see if it is believable. See if you believe the story of the men of Fobbing when you have answered the questions.

1 *Places in the story*

(a) Fobbing, Corringham and Stanford are mentioned in the story. Are these real villages in Essex or have they been made up? Look at the map on page 32.

(b) We are told that Sir Robert Belknap arrived in Brentwood to punish the rebels a few days after John Bampton reported them to the King's Council in London.

   (i) How far is Brentwood from London?

   (ii) Could Belknap have got to Brentwood a few days after Bampton left? Give reasons for your answer.

2 *People in the story*

(a) The chronicle tells us one villager's name.

   (i) What was the villager's name?

   (ii) Is it likely that the writer would have known this villager's name when he does not seem to know the names of any of the others? Give reasons for your answer.

(b) We are told that John Bampton owned land in Essex and that Sir Robert Belknap was an important judge. Is it likely that the writer would have made up these names? Give reasons for your answer.

3 *The events in the story*

We are told that a group of villagers

   made the King's tax collector leave Essex,

   defied a judge,

   murdered six men.

Consider what the story tells us about each of these events. Do you believe what we are told about the villagers' behaviour? Give reasons for your answer.

What do you think?

Consider everything you have learnt from studying the story of the men of Fobbing. Which of these statements is the most accurate?

   The story is probably true.

   The story may be true.

   The story cannot be true.

Give reasons for your answer.

Understanding what happened

1 Rewrite these events in the correct order:

   The King's Council sends Sir Robert Belknap to Brentwood to investigate disturbances in Essex.

   Men from Essex join villagers from other counties and march to London to put their case to the King.

   Parliament charges three groats a head to pay for the wars against France.

   The men of Fobbing murder people who have informed against them and drive away Sir Robert Belknap.

   Essex villagers claim they have paid the tax and drive out the tax collector.

2 Copy the statement below that you think is correct:

The men of Fobbing claimed that they had paid the poll tax of 1381 so they refused to pay any extra money.

The men of Fobbing claimed that they had paid the poll tax of 1377 so they did not see why they should pay another poll tax in 1381.

3 (a) How many people died in disturbances in Essex before Sir Robert Belknap returned to London?
(b) What information did the villagers make Belknap give them that led to six murders?

What do you think?
Why did the rebels decide to go to the King for help?

Further work

Writing

1 The men of Fobbing's first violent action was to drive Bampton away from the court room in Brentwood.
(a) Make a list of all of the acts of violence that they committed.
(b) Copy the statement below that you think is correct:

The Fobbing villagers were violent, dangerous men.
Some of the Fobbing villagers were violent, dangerous men.
Give reasons for your answer.

2 Write the report that *either* John Bampton *or* Sir Robert Belknap might have given to the Council in London, explaining why he had failed to complete the work he was ordered to do in Brentwood.

3 'What kind of a place is Fobbing and what kind of people live there?'
Write the answer that two of these people might have given to the question above:
Thomas the Baker
one of Belknap's soldiers
one of Bampton's guards
the Lord Treasurer, after he heard Belknap's report

Drawing

1 Copy the picture of the tally stick on page 31. Write one or two sentences under your drawing explaining what an official at the Treasury could learn from a tally stick.

2 Study the picture of a judge's brass on page 32. Draw a picture of Sir Robert Belknap, dressed in his robes, taking evidence from the jurors at Brentwood. Write a sentence explaining why it was dangerous for the jurors to give evidence.

3 Draw three pictures showing how the villagers' protest against the poll tax began peacefully and ended violently. Write a sentence under each picture to explain what is happening. Give a title to your set of pictures.

Drama

1 (a) Write the speech that Thomas the Baker might have made to the men of Corringham and Stanford, urging them to support the Fobbing villagers.
Things to write about:
The reasons why you are determined not to pay the tax.
What you propose to do to make Bampton listen to you.
What you propose to do if Bampton refuses to listen to you.
(b) Choose someone to make the speech to the class, who form the audience of Essex villagers. At the end of the speech, villagers may make comments on the plan and offer suggestions for discussion.
(c) Take a vote on whether or not to follow Thomas's plan.

More people, more food

In 1300 there was no sign of a rebellion in England. The population had been increasing, there was work for everyone, and life in most villages seemed settled and peaceful.

Between 1066 and 1300 the population of England trebled. To feed the increased numbers English farmers had to produce more food. They did this in various ways.

In 1066 many villages had two huge arable fields. Each year one field was cultivated while the other was left fallow—without a crop—for the soil to rest and get back its fertility. So only half the land was used at a time. When demand for food began to grow the villagers split the two fields into three. They sowed spring corn in one field, autumn wheat in another, and left the third fallow. Now only a third of the land was left unused instead of half, and food production increased.

If they were still short of space to grow corn, the villagers cut down some of the forest and cultivated the land on which the trees had grown. Sometimes they ploughed up some pasture and meadow. This meant that they could grow more corn, but could not keep so many animals. They used animal dung to fertilise their arable fields. If they got rid of too many animals they would not have enough manure to go round, and the arable land would gradually become less fertile. So they did not plough up too much pasture.

As the population continued to grow, people looked round the country to find new sites to set up villages. All the best places had already been taken, but they often found room for a village on bleak hills where the soil was thin and poor, or on heavy, undrained land in the valleys. If they thought there was a chance that the ground would produce reasonable crops they set to work. They cleared, drained, ploughed and built until they had established a new village with its houses, streets, fields, pasture and meadow. Because the soil was poor they had to work hard to grow enough food to live on, but fortunately the climate in the thirteenth century was usually mild and pleasant, and helped their crops.

Crops and animals

Even on good land, crops in the Middle Ages were poor compared with today, and the animals were very small. Barley produced about 5 grains for every one sown, wheat 4, and oats 2 or 3. A farmer today would expect to get about six or seven times as much as this.

A cow gave between 500 and 600 litres of milk a year. Today a dairy cow gives ten times as much. In 1300 a fleece of wool weighed 500 grams, or even less, compared with 2 kilograms today.

Crops and animals did badly partly because the soil was not properly fertilised, and the animals were not well fed. Sheep and cattle had to forage for themselves on the pasture and the fallow field. But many of them were also sick, for diseases spread quickly among them as they grazed together on the common pasture, and nobody knew how to cure or prevent them.

	Year One	Year Two	Year Three
Field 1	Fallow	Autumn wheat	Spring corn
Field 2	Autumn wheat	Spring corn	Fallow
Field 3	Spring corn	Fallow	Autumn wheat

▲ The rotation of crops on a three-field system. Farmers sowed the autumn wheat in the field that had been left fallow, so that they had plenty of time to prepare the land before sowing

Study

Feeding a growing population

Draw the diagram of the village and its fields below. ⑤

1 (a) Copy the statement that you think is correct:

Three times as many people lived in England in 1300 as in 1066. ①

Three times as many people lived in England in 1066 as in 1300.

(b) The villagers who live in the village shown in the diagram have reorganised the open fields where they grow their grain. Read the section headed 'More people, more food', on page 35. Explain

(i) why farmers grew more food, ①

(ii) how farmers grew more food. ⑥

2 (a) Name the tenant who (i) lives in the original village and grows his crops on strips of land scattered through the open fields, ⓪

(ii) lives in a newly built hut and grows his crops on a block of newly ploughed land. ①

(b) Which areas marked on the diagram can be used by both tenants? ③

3 Read the section on 'Crops and animals' on page 35.

(a) Give an example to show that, compared with modern farmers, medieval farmers produced less grain from the same amount of seed. ②

(b) Give an example to show that farmers today can produce more meat from their animals than medieval farmers could. ②

(c) Give two reasons why animals were often sick or badly nourished. ②

OUT OF 24

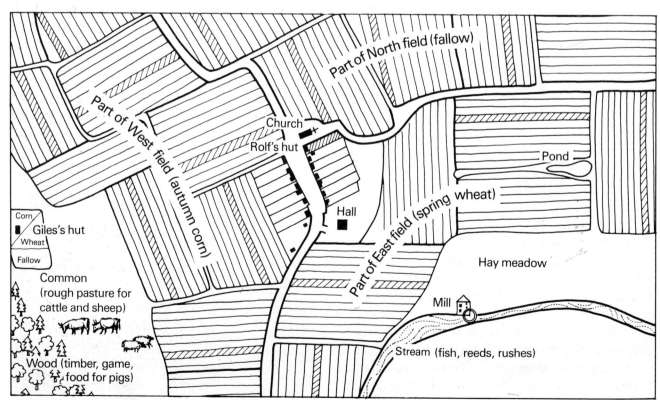

▲ A diagram of the three-field system, showing part of each of the fields. The shaded strips in each field were farmed by Rolf. All villagers could use the Common and the Hay meadow

Life in the village

The villein

Most of the land in a village was owned by the lord of the manor. He kept some, called the demesne, for himself. The rest of it was cultivated by tenants who rented it out from him. Some of them were free men who paid him rent, but most were villeins.

A villein held his land on strict conditions. He could not leave the village without his lord's permission. He paid a small rent in money and every week he or one of his family had to go to work on the lord's demesne for a set number of days—usually one or two. This was called 'week work'. In addition he had to do 'boon work'—a number of days at ploughing and harvest time.

This work was carefully organised. Every week the bailiff, who was employed by the lord of the manor to run the demesne for him, decided how many villeins he needed. He told the reeve, who was elected by the villeins to organise their work for them. The reeve then shared the work out among the villeins.

In addition to rent and work, the villein had to pay various dues to the lord of the manor. Every Easter he had to hand over a set number of eggs, and at Christmas a few chickens. When he took over his land he had to give the lord a 'heriot', usually his best cow. He paid another tax, 'merchet', when his daughter married. The lord also had the right to levy a tax known as 'tallage' whenever he liked.

The villein had to pay taxes to the Church as well. The biggest was 'tithe', which was a tenth of everything he produced. When he took over his land the Church had the right to his second-best cow, and whenever any of his family were christened, married or buried he had to pay a fee.

A villein had to make enough from his land to feed his family and pay all his dues to the lord of the manor and the Church. The amount of land he might hold varied enormously from place to place, but was usually between 15 and 30 hectares.

This land was scattered in long narrow strips over the three fields of the village. In addition, the villein had the right to graze a few animals on the common pasture, and a share of the hay from the meadow.

The villein's house and garden

Most villeins lived with their families in small houses, often only 3 metres by 5 metres. The walls were made of interlaced branches covered with mud and fixed to a framework of wooden posts driven into the ground. There was usually only one room. The floor was earth, with a stone hearth in the middle. There was no chimney and the only window was a small, square opening in the wall without any glass. The roof was thatched. These houses were draughty, dirty, dark and damp. They were often overrun with rats, mice and fleas. But they were cheap and easy to build.

Villeins' houses were poorly furnished. Most had a bed, a bench or chair, a couple of stools and perhaps a trestle table. For cooking the villein and his family used a bronze pot which stood on an iron tripod over the fire. The villeins ate from wooden or earthenware plates and bowls.

A villein usually had about a quarter of a hectare of land attached to his house. He could do as he pleased with it. Most kept a few hens or geese, and grew peas and beans. A few grew flax to make linen. Some had fruit trees and kept bees.

▲ One of the villeins' jobs was threshing the corn to separate the ears of grain from the straw. They did this by beating the corn with flails. It was hard work

▼ In some places the shape of the medieval strips can still be seen today, in the form of ridges and furrows in grass fields

Villeins depended on their families to help them. Their wives had to cook, clean, look after the children and feed the animals. Often, when the villeins had to go to work on the demesne, they left jobs half-finished on their own land. Then their wives or their older children had to go and finish them off, while the villeins themselves were at work on the lord of the manor's land.

A villein's food

Villeins had a very simple diet. Most of them lived on coarse dark bread and stew thickened with oatmeal and flavoured with a few vegetables and a little meat. Sometimes they had eggs, and they drank water, milk and weak ale. 'Cheese,' said one writer in the fourteenth century, 'was like a feast to them.'

To have enough energy to do their work the villeins needed to eat huge quantities of bread—about 2 kilograms a day. Many of them did not get as much as this, and were weak and did not have much energy. By today's standards they died young. Very few reached the age of fifty.

A villein's life was always hard, but at the beginning of the fourteenth century it was particularly difficult. As land was scarce, lords of the manor could afford to treat their villeins very harshly. If they complained, there were plenty of men who had no land and who would be only too pleased to take their places.

Study

Food and shelter

Class activity

A peasant family's hut

Most peasant families lived in one-roomed huts, measuring about 3 metres by 5 metres.

1 Measure 3 metres by 5 metres along two walls of your classroom. Would a hut have been larger or smaller than your classroom? No

2 How many square metres did the floor of the hut cover?

3 If the hearth covered about 1 square metre, what area of floor space was left for these items of furniture?

    a stool   a trestle table   a bed

4 Five or more people may have lived in the hut. What might they have done with the furniture to give themselves more room, (a) during the day, (b) at night?

A peasant family's food

Compare your answers to the following questions.

1 How many slices of bread do you eat (a) in a day, (b) in a week?

2 If each slice of bread weighs about 25 grams, how many grams of bread do you eat (a) in a day, (b) in a week?

3 A villein ate about 2 kilograms of bread a day. Is this more than you eat

    in a day,
    in 3 days,
    in a week?

A peasant's lifespan

Compare your answers to the following questions.

1 How many relatives have you who are aged

    60–70 years
    70–80 years
    80–90 years?

2 In the fourteenth century, very few people reached the age of fifty. Why did (a) their living conditions, (b) their diet cause them to die young, compared with people in Britain today?

OUT OF 20

On your own

1 (a) Copy this diagram of a peasant family's hut.

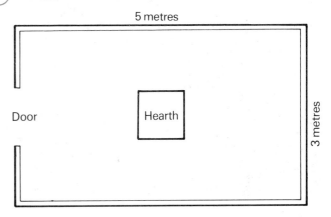

2 metres   5 metres   Door   Hearth   3 metres

(b) Add these items of furniture to your diagram:

    a stool   a trestle table   a bed

(c) Study the section on a villein's food on page 38. Give examples of (i) two kinds of meat, (ii) two kinds of vegetables, that might have gone into the cooking pot on the hearth. Why was it so difficult to keep the hut clean and dry?

A peasant's duties

1 (a) Copy this table.

A VILLEIN'S DUES

Time of year	Dues paid to the lord
Spring	Several days' ploughing
_____	Eggs
Harvest	_____
_____	Chicken

(b) Study the section on a villein's rent and work. (i) Fill in the gaps in each list, and (ii) write a sentence explaining what 'week work' was.

2 Under the heading: 'Taxes', list the taxes that the villein paid to his lord and the Church.

→

What do you think?
Why was it essential for a villein to sow his crops and harvest the grain, but hard for him to do so?
3 (a) Why was a villein unable (i) to leave his village, (ii) to complain if his rent was high?
(b) Why was a lord able (i) to make money from his demesne, (ii) to pay low wages?

(c) Explain why each of these men was important in the village: (i) the bailiff, (ii) the baker.

What do you think?
Which of the men mentioned in question 3(c) was most likely to reach the age of fifty? Give reasons for your answer.

Rich and poor

The lord of the manor

Most lords of the manor were very well off in 1300. The growing population needed somewhere to live, and land on which to produce food. Lords of the manor who had land to let found that they could demand a high rent. They could also get a high price for the food they grew on their demesne land. So they did well.

The lord of the manor lived much better than his villeins. He had a large house with a big dining hall and several other rooms. Often his house was protected by a moat and a wooden palisade. He ate better than his tenants. He had more meat and fish, and drank wine or mead rather than ale.

Many lords had more than one manor. Usually they visited each one in turn, but if one was a long way from the rest, or if the lord was away on important business at court, or fighting for the King, he would not have time to call in regularly. Then he employed a steward to live on his manor and take his place.

One of the lord's most important duties was to make sure that his tenants lived peacefully and obeyed the law. So he or his steward regularly held a court at the manor house where they settled quarrels among the tenants, fined villeins who did not do their week work or their boon work properly, and punished those who had broken the law. To help keep order the lord appointed a village constable.

The priest

Nearly every village had a priest who said Mass at the village church, heard confessions, and christened, married and buried the villagers. He was usually appointed by the lord of the manor. He had some land to farm, called the 'glebe', and also received tithes and fees. So in a large village with rich land he got a good living. But if the population was small and the soil infertile he had a poor life. As a rule the priest was the only person in the village who could read or write.

Craftsmen and cottagers

Some people in the village owned little or no land. A few were craftsmen like the smith. They worked full time at their trades. Others were poor cottagers who hired themselves out as labourers. At ploughing and harvest time they could always get work, but at other times of the year it was not so easy, and they often went hungry for weeks at a time. When the harvest was poor and food was dear, they starved.

▲ The smith uses pincers to hold a piece of hot iron as he and his assistant hammer it on the anvil

Study

Use your imagination

In the first quarter of the fourteenth century life became harder. There were several cold wet summers and poor harvests. In these years the death rate rose. Few people actually starved to death, but because they did not have enough to eat, many were too weak to resist tuberculosis, influenza, pneumonia and dysentery. When food was short they were also tempted to eat rotting meat or mildewed grain, and poisoned themselves. The poor suffered most, and those who lived in villages on infertile soil or windy hills died first.

1 'Often famished with hunger, and wretched with ... cold sleepless nights, when [she] gets up to rock the cradle cramped in a corner, and rises before dawn ... to wash and mend ... and peel rushes for [her] rush lights'.
This is how William Langland, who lived in the fourteenth century, described a village woman's life in winter. Write an account of her life during a severe winter.
Things to write about:
The hut that Kit, a village woman, lived in with her husband, Walter, and their first child, Giles,
Their life in winter when food was scarce,
How the baby caught a fever and Kit nursed him, and whether he lived or died.
(Think of a time when you have been cold, hungry and worried.)

2 In William Langland's poem, *Piers Plowman*, Sir Roger Godfrey, a knight who wants to help to put things right in England, offers to learn to plough and labour with his peasants in the fields. Piers replies: 'I'll sweat and toil for both of us as long as I live. But you must promise to ... protect me from thieves and wasters ... and you'll have to hunt down all the hares and foxes that break down my hedges, and tame falcons to kill the wild birds that crop my wheat.'

Write an account of Sir Godfrey, who has just inherited his land, going on a tour of inspection.
Things to write about:
Sir Godfrey rides around his land, watching his peasants working.
He meets Bertram the Reeve and asks his advice on how to win the peasants' respect.
How Bertram advises Sir Godfrey, and whether his lord follows his advice.
(Think of a time when you have wanted advice and what you did when you were given it.)

3 The poem *Piers Plowman* begins with Roger the Priest: 'One summer season ... I set out to roam far and wide, hoping to hear of marvels. But on a morning in May, among the Malvern Hills, a strange thing happened to me ... I was tired out by my wanderings, and as I lay down to rest by the side of a stream ... it sounded so pleasant that I fell asleep. And I dreamed a marvellous dream.'
Write an account of Roger the Priest, who wants to help the poor, and leaves his home to see what is happening in the world.
Things to write about:
Roger, a priest, thinks it is wrong for bishops to make so much money when most people are poor.
He sets out to wander through the countryside and think about his ideas for improving the life of the poor people.
He meets Jack the Shepherd, who thinks that peasants and gentlemen should be more equal.
Roger describes to Jack the kind of England he wants to live in, and his plans for putting his ideas into action.
(Think of how you have discussed ideas that you think are important with someone who agrees with you.)

The Black Death

In 1346 travellers told of a new and terrible disease raging in western China. It took three different forms. Some victims developed a high fever with frequent vomiting. Painful swellings known as buboes appeared in their groins and armpits. Then black and purple blotches appeared on their skin, and within a few days they died. In the second form of the disease the victim's lungs rotted away. He coughed up blood, and died within two days. The third form was the quickest of all. People suddenly collapsed and died as if they had drunk poison.

In 1346 the disease seemed a long way away, but in 1347 it reached the southern coasts of Italy and France. By 1348 it was raging in Paris, and later in the summer traders crossing the Channel carried it to the south coast of England.

Illness in the Middle Ages

In the Middle Ages people did not know how diseases were caused. Some thought gases in the air made people ill. Some believed that illness was sent by God as a punishment for people's sins, or was caused by the planets moving in the sky. Many were sure that witches could cause disease by putting spells on people.

Doctors had various ways of trying to cure or prevent diseases, depending on what they thought the causes were. Some told their patients to sniff aromatic herbs, believing that they purified the air. Some doctors prayed, or used charms and spells. Many believed in herbal medicines. Usually they chose a herb because of its appearance. Wood-sorrel is heart-shaped, so doctors used it to treat heart disease. They gave yellow juice of celandine to people whose skin had turned yellow from jaundice. These 'cures' rarely did any good.

Today we know that Bubonic Plague, the disease which spread over Europe between 1347 and 1349, is carried by rats and by the fleas which live on them. The Plague kills the rats, and the fleas leave their cooling bodies to find somewhere warm to live. They jump onto people passing by, bite them to feed on their blood and in doing so inject the germ into their bloodstream. If the disease attacks the lungs, every time the sick person coughs he pumps thousands of germs into the air, and anyone who breathes them in may also be infected. But in the fourteenth century all this was unknown. The Plague seemed to be a 'rootless phantom without mercy' roaming the streets and fields.

▲ A fourteenth-century picture showing people crowding into a churchyard in Tournai in Belgium.

They carry coffins containing the bodies of Plague victims

The Plague in Britain

Gradually the Plague spread over the whole of Britain. People were terrified. The disease made its victims stink, and in any case everybody knew that if they went close to the sick and dying they risked catching the Plague themselves. So they kept away. The Bishop of Bath and Wells complained that priests were unwilling to visit Plague victims to hear their confessions. In Scotland a chronicler wrote that people were so frightened of infection that they would not visit their own parents lying on their death-bed.

The poor suffered most. With the whole family crammed into one room they could not avoid close contact if one of them fell ill. Their houses were almost certain to be infested by rats and fleas and, as most of the poor were villeins, they were not allowed to leave the villages in which they lived. So they had to stay, suffer and die. The rich had larger, cleaner houses and could travel as they wished. This meant that fewer of them died.

The Plague killed about a third of the population of Britain. In Bristol so many people died that the living were hardly able to bury the dead, and there were so few passers-by that grass grew high in the main streets of the town. At Rochester men and women carried their children's bodies on their shoulders to the churchyard and threw them into a common pit. This pit stank so badly that people hardly dared even to walk past the churchyard. In many places existing cemeteries were too small, and new ones had to be opened.

In London the Plague killed two archbishops in one year, the Abbot of Westminster and about 30,000 of the population of 100,000. At St Alban's Abbey forty-seven out of a hundred monks died and at Winchester the disease reduced the town's population from 8,000 to 4,000. At Ashwell in Hertfordshire in 1350 somebody scrawled a message on the church wall. It read: 'Wretched, terrible, destructive year. The remnants of the people alone remain.' In the north, when the time came for tenants to pay their rents to the Bishop of Durham, no one came from West Thickley 'because they are all dead'.

By the end of 1350 the worst of the Plague was over. In some places it seems to have

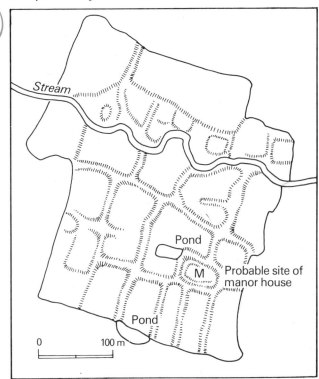

▼ A plan of the remaining banks and ditches on the site of the deserted village of Hamilton, near Leicester. Once ten families lived here. It was deserted between 1400 and 1500

brought life to a standstill for a time. In Devon the wool trade ceased, the tin mines closed down, and building work on the nave of Exeter Cathedral was stopped. At Wyville, a little village in Leicestershire, the land lay uncultivated 'for want of tenants after the Plague', and at Hemingborough in Yorkshire the cattle wandered as they pleased over the pasture because 'the herdsmen were lying in the churchyard'.

Deserted villages

Most villages recovered quickly from the Plague. There were some vacant holdings, but there were still enough villeins to till most of the fields. A few villages on poor sites were completely deserted. Others were left with very few people. There were further outbreaks of Plague in 1361, 1368, 1371, 1375, 1390 and 1405. These killed fewer people than the first outbreak in 1348, but the population continued to shrink, and people moved away from villages on poor sites until a large number of them were deserted. Many have remained uninhabited ever since.

Study

The site of a deserted village

The sites of deserted villages can still be seen in the countryside today. Usually the line of the village street shows as a wide grassy ditch with rectangular plots on each side. Sometimes traces of the manor house with its moat can be seen. Occasionally the church still stands, or there may be fragments of its wall poking out of the soil. Rabbits burrowing on these sites may bring fragments of medieval pottery to the surface, while the strips of open fields surrounding the village often show up as long ridges and furrows in nearby pastures.

▼ Today the site of Hamilton is just a lumpy, grass-covered field

1 Draw the plan of Hamilton on page 43.
2 Look carefully at the plan and then write the following in what you think is the correct place on the plan:

cottage   yard or garden
open field

3 Look at the photograph of Hamilton, and consider the information given above. Make a list of three or more clues that you might find in a country district that would make you suspect that you had found the site of a deserted village.

How many people died?

		Key
Population of England and Wales in 1349	☺ ☺ ☺	☺ = 1 million
Deaths in 1349	♱	♱ = 1 million

(The figures given above are rough estimates.)

1 Copy the table above.
(a) What was the total population of England and Wales in 1349?
(b) What proportion of the population died in 1349?

(c) Draw a diagram to show the total population of England and Wales when the Plague ended.

Place	Population	Deaths
St Alban's Abbey	100 monks	47
City of Winchester	8,000	4,000

The figures above were recorded by people who lived in 1349.

2 (a) The figures for St Alban's Abbey are probably accurate. Why would it have been possible for monks to keep accurate figures?

(b) The figures given for Winchester are probably a rough estimate. Why may it have been difficult for the townspeople to count the number of deaths taking place accurately?

(c) A figure that has been rounded off, for example, the number of deaths given for Winchester, is usually a rough estimate. If a monk at St Alban's had rounded off the death at the abbey to the nearest 10, what number would he have given?

3 *Historical demographers* try to work out how many people died in a particular town in 1349. They base their calculations on clues such as:

The number of wills the rich men of the town made in 1349,

The number of skeletons found in a mass grave dated about 1349.

The figures that a demographer worked out from the clues given above would *not* help us know:

(a) The total number of deaths in the town in 1349,

(b) The total number of deaths from the Black Death in 1349.

Explain why not.

Unrest after the Black Death

Wages and prices

The Plague affected wages and prices. There were fewer labourers than before, and they began to demand higher wages, particularly at harvest time. If a landowner refused to pay, his workers left his crops in the fields and went to work for someone else. Most landowners paid, and within a year wages doubled.

At the same time prices fell. People were frightened to go to market, and the landowners could not sell their produce. The price of oxen was halved, and the price of wool fell to its lowest level since 1300. Rents fell, too because there was no longer a shortage of land.

The Statute of Labourers, 1351

Landowners were very hard-hit. They got less for their produce and their land, but had to pay higher wages to their workers. They were so badly off that the Parliament of 1351 made a new law, known as the Statute of Labourers.

This law reduced wages to the level they had been before the Plague, and bound labourers to serve their masters for at least a year at a time. Landowners did their best to enforce the new law. In 1351, 7,500 people were fined in Essex alone for paying labourers too much. Most of them were peasants who had hired one or two labourers to help them.

Peasants and labourers hated the new law, and continued to break it. Between 1377 and 1379 70 per cent of the people brought before the justices of the peace in Essex were accused of breaking the Statute of Labourers. In the poem *Piers Plowman* the ploughman curses 'the King and all his Council for passing such laws'. So peasants had good reason to dislike courts of law, lawyers and the government.

▼ After the Black Death the wages of labourers on the lands of the Bishop of Winchester rose sharply

Year	Average wage (old pence per day)
1301–1310	1.49
1311–1320	1.87
1321–1330	1.84
1331–1340	1.78
1341–1350	1.86
1351–1360	2.85
1361–1370	3.25
1371–1380	3.19
1381–1390	3.35
1391–1400	3.30

The villeins

After the Plague, life was very different for many villeins. While the disease was raging, some escaped from their villages and went to towns where they easily found work and somewhere to live. Others made their way to nearby villages and took on land as free tenants. They were better off than they had been.

Villeins who stayed in their villages were often worse off than they had been before the Plague. There were few of them, and to make up for this, many landowners tried to make them do more boon work and week work than before. The villeins complained and argued. In some places they banded together, refused to work and even threatened their bailiffs. Parliament tried to prevent this by passing an Act allowing landowners to arrest any of their villeins who seemed to be 'rebellious' and to imprison them for as long as they liked.

If the villeins now tried to escape from their villages landowners hunted them down and brought them back. When labourers were in short supply, villeins were valuable.

The wealthy landowners

By 1380 many peasants hated all landowners. The most unpopular was the King's uncle, John of Gaunt, Duke of Lancaster. John was the richest man in the country. He owned estates all over England, had land in France, and claimed to be King of Castile in Spain. He had about 200 attendants, including barons and knights. His house in London was a magnificent castle called the Savoy.

When peasants thought of John of Gaunt with his power, wealth, courtiers and palaces, they felt jealous and angry. They knew that his wealth came from rents and taxes which they and people like them had to pay. Why should landowners like John of Gaunt have so much while ordinary peasants had so little? Some said it was God's will, but others disagreed. They said that when God had created the first man and woman he had made them equal, and they quoted a rhyme:

When Adam delved and Eve span
Who was then the gentleman?

Many peasants also hated and despised rich churchmen. The Church of England owned huge estates. Bishops and the abbots of rich monasteries sat in Parliament with the other great landowners, and lived in luxury. The peasants respected monks and priests who, like Christ and his disciples, lived in poverty, but they had no time for rich and powerful churchmen.

When peasants paid their rents, dues and taxes they thought bitterly of the landowners and bishops, and wondered how much of the money would find its way into their pockets. So in 1381 there were good reasons why peasants flocked to join the men of Fobbing on their march on London.

Study

Wages and prices in the fourteenth century

Labourers' wages and the law

Historians agree that after 1349 there was a trend towards a higher standard of living in Britain. That is to say, most people who survived the Plague were better off than they had been before. One reason for this was that many labourers were now paid higher wages.

Trends in wage rates

Study the table of wages on page 46. This shows the average daily wage paid to labourers who worked on a manor owned by the Bishop of Winchester.

1 (a) What was the average daily wage in (i) 1301, (ii) 1400?
   (b) Was the trend of wages between 1301 and 1400 upward or downward?
2 The Statute of Labourers was made law in 1351. It stated that it was against the law to pay a workman more wages than he had received before the Plague.
   (a) How many pence a day did the average wage rise between 1350 and 1360?
   (b) By law, how many pence a day should the average wage have been in 1360?
   (c) Did the Bishop of Winchester obey or disobey the law?
3 Study the passage headed 'The Statute of Labourers' on page 45.
   (a) What evidence from Essex shows that many people in this county disobeyed the Statute of Labourers soon after it was made law?
   (b) What evidence shows that the Statute was still being broken in Essex more than twenty years later?
   (c) Essex is in the south of England. The lands of the Bishop of Winchester were in the south. The evidence from these two places gives us *examples* of the trend towards higher wages. Explain why it does not give us *proof* of the trend.

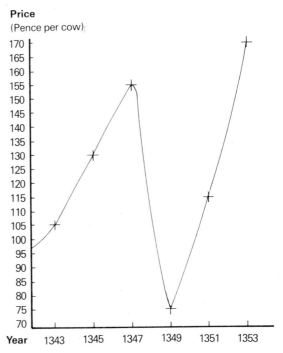

▼ The price of cattle sold at Cheddington in Buckinghamshire fell in 1349, but quickly rose again

Prices at the market

Study the graph. It shows the prices paid for cattle sold at Cheddington market in Buckinghamshire between 1343 and 1353.

1 (a) How many pence per head did cattle cost in (i) 1343, (ii) 1353?
   (b) Is the overall trend of prices between 1343 and 1353 upward or downward?
   (c) Which years do not show this trend?
2 (a) Why may fewer people have gone to the market to buy cattle in 1349?
   (b) How do we know that *some* cattle were bought that year?
   (c) Why did the men selling cattle have to accept a low price for them?
3 (a) In which year did prices rise sharply?
   (b) Why may more people have thought it was safe to go to market by that time?
   (c) Many peasants and landowners needed to build up their herds again. Explain why the men selling cattle could raise their prices. →

Who was then the gentleman?

▲ A fourteenth-century peasant couple

▲ A gentleman and his lady

1 (a) Draw the picture of the peasant and his wife.

(b) Copy the rhyme beginning 'When Adam delved . . .' on page 46.

2 (a) Draw the picture of the gentleman and his lady.

(b) Only men who owned land could call themselves gentlemen. Rewrite the rhyme on page 46 in your own words. (You need not make them rhyme.)

3 (a) Draw a picture showing a peasant leader urging the peasants to rebel.

(b) Write the speech the peasant leader might have made, declaring that John of Gaunt used his power to make himself even richer and not to help his country.

The Peasants' Revolt

The rebels march on London

At the beginning of June 1381 the men of Essex began their march on London. They went to Temple Cressing, a manor owned by the Knights of St John. The commander of the knights was Sir Robert Hales, the country's treasurer. The rebels broke into the manor house, which was well stocked with food. They ate all the food, drank three barrels of wine, and then burnt the house to the ground. They went on to Coggershall, where the Sheriff of Essex lived, and burnt his house.

Tyler and the rebels in Kent

The men of Kent were also on the move. A large band of them surrounded Rochester Castle where a runaway villein was imprisoned. After a few hours the constable of the castle, Sir John Newton, surrendered and was taken prisoner. The triumphant rebels then marched on to Maidstone, where they found a new leader, named Wat Tyler.

Nobody knows anything about Wat Tyler before the day when he joined the rebels in 1381. He must have been bold and determined, for within a few hours he had taken command.

He led his men to Canterbury and burst into the cathedral. He told the monks that very soon they would have to choose a new archbishop because the present one would be executed. He then captured the Sheriff of Kent and burnt all the records of his court. Tyler also opened the archbishop's prison at Canterbury and released John Ball, a priest who had been imprisoned for preaching sermons attacking the wealth and power of the clergy.

John Ball supported the peasants, and told them they were quite right to march on London to demand their freedom and the punishment of the landowners who were advising the King.

The rebels in London

The rebels reach London

Encouraged by John Ball the Kentish rebels moved quickly to London, and on 11 June they and the men from Essex camped just outside the city walls. They sent Sir John Newton to tell the King that they wanted to meet him, and on the morning of 12 June the young King Richard set out from the Tower of London in his royal barge to sail down the river Thames to Greenwich, where there was a huge crowd of rebels waiting.

When his barge came into sight the rebels began to shout and cheer so loudly that the King's advisers were frightened. They ordered the barge to return to the Tower.

The rebels then sent a message demanding the execution of John of Gaunt and fifteen others. Richard refused, but promised to meet the rebels on 17 June. They had already looted the suburb of Southwark, destroyed the Archbishop of Canterbury's house at Lambeth, and burnt all his documents. But both these places were outside the city walls, and Richard took it for granted that the rebels would not be able to get into London itself. He was wrong.

▲ This fourteenth-century picture of the Peasants' Revolt shows John Ball on horseback, with Wat Tyler on the left. The peasants carry the cross of George and the Royal Standard. The picture shows the peasants wearing armour, but in fact they did not

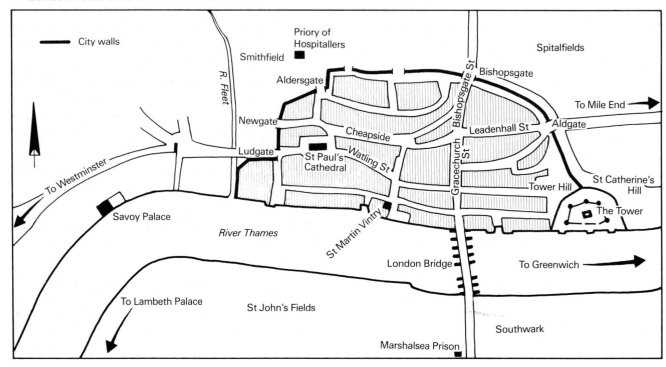

Map labels: City walls · Priory of Hospitallers · Spitalfields · Smithfield · R. Fleet · Aldersgate · Bishopsgate St · Bishopsgate · To Mile End · Newgate · Cheapside · Leadenhall St · Aldgate · To Westminster · Ludgate · St Paul's Cathedral · Watling St · Gracechurch St · Tower Hill · St Catherine's Hill · The Tower · Savoy Palace · St Martin Vintry · River Thames · London Bridge · To Greenwich · To Lambeth Palace · St John's Fields · Southwark · Marshalsea Prison

Fire and slaughter

Early in the morning of 13 June the rebels somehow entered the city. Some went out to John of Gaunt's Savoy palace, and broke in. They took all the furniture and linen, heaped them up in the great hall and set fire to them. Some of them, not realising what they were doing, hurled three barrels of gunpowder onto the fire. The barrels blew up, and the Savoy was reduced to a blackened ruin. John of Gaunt was away in the north of England. If he had been in London the rebels would have killed him.

The rebels also attacked and destroyed all the property in London owned by the Knights of St John. They broke into the Bishop of Durham's house, went down into the cellars, brought out barrels of wine, and drank their fill. Some then tried to break into the King's treasury at Westminster, but the guards drove them away.

The King meets the rebels at Mile End

The King's Council realised that the rebels might destroy the whole city. So on the morning of 14 June the King, with William Walworth, the Mayor of London, a few of his Council and some soldiers, rode to Mile End, where most of the rebels from Essex and Hertfordshire had gathered.

The King and his ministers were frightened, and were prepared to promise almost anything if in return the rebels would return home. The rebels drove a hard bargain. They forced the King to grant them a pardon for rebelling against him. He had to give them permission to arrest anybody they thought was a traitor, and he declared that all the villeins among them were to be freed at once. The rebels were delighted, and many of them set off for home.

Tyler's men in London

Meanwhile Wat Tyler and some of the men from Kent went to the Tower of London. The constable of the Tower did not know what to do. The King was at Mile End, and the rebels told him they had permission to go in and arrest any traitors they found. Eventually the constable let them in. The rebels searched the whole place. One made his way into the royal bedchamber, and thrust his sword through the King's bed. Others found Archbishop Sudbury of Canterbury, Treasurer Hales and John of Gaunt's doctor, hiding. They took them out onto Tower Green and chopped their heads off.

Then the rebels left the Tower and went back into the city. Many were drunk. They took the heads of the men they had executed and stuck them up over London Bridge. Then they searched for foreigners. In the church of St Martin Vintry they found 35 Flemish merchants. They dragged them out and beheaded them. They broke into foreigner's houses and looted them. Anyone who tried to stop them was killed. All that day and far into the night the streets rang with the shouts of the rebels and the screams of their victims. An official wrote that 'there was hardly a street in the city in which there were not bodies lying. Also some of the houses in the city were pulled down'.

The next day some rebels entered Westminster Abbey and found Richard Imworth, warden of Marshalsea Prison. He was well known for ill-treating prisoners, and had gone to the abbey, thinking that the rebels would not dare to harm him in this holy place. He was wrong. They dragged him out and killed him.

The meeting at Smithfield

To try to get the rebels out of London, King Richard issued a proclamation inviting them to meet him just outside the city at Smithfield. When Richard, the mayor and a few courtiers arrived they found Wat Tyler and the men from Kent waiting for them. The King hoped that by making a few promises, as he had at Mile End, he would be able to persuade the peasants to go home. But Tyler would not leave unless Richard promised to change the whole system of law, take all the church land to give to the people, and do away with all but one of the bishops.

Richard would not give in to these demands. Tyler argued with him. He shocked the courtiers by refusing to take his hat off in the King's presence. He also spat on the ground and gulped down a few mouthfuls of beer. One of Richard's followers said in a loud voice that Wat was 'the greatest thief and robber in all Kent'. Wat drew his dagger and tried to attack the courtier. The mayor held Wat back. Tyler struggled, the mayor stabbed him in the neck, and another courtier drew his sword, ran Wat through the body and killed him.

When the peasants saw Tyler fall some of them bent their bows and prepared to shoot at the courtiers. But Richard spurred his horse forward towards them. 'Will you shoot your King?' he shouted. 'I am your leader, follow me.' The rebels were confused and uncertain. Most of them did not know exactly what had happened. So when the young King offered to lead them away they thought it best to follow. Richard eventually handed them over to two knights who saw them over London Bridge and back into Kent. The Revolt was over.

▲ Richard II. He became unpopular, and was deposed in 1399

▲ This picture shows two events. On the left Wat Tyler is being killed. On the right Richard II is riding over to the peasants telling them to follow him

The government and the rebels

Copy the map of London on page 50 into your book.

1 (a) Rewrite the list below in the order in which the events took place:

The rebels enter the city.

The Savoy Palace and other buildings are destroyed.

Richard and the rebels meet at Smithfield—Tyler is killed.

Richard and the rebels meet at Mile End—some rebels go home.

Royal officials and foreign merchants are murdered.

Southwark and Lambeth are looted.

(b) How did the rebels show their hatred for (i) the Archbishop of Canterbury, (ii) John of Gaunt?

2 (a) Copy the table headed 'The rebels meet the King' and fill in the spaces.

(b) Give examples of the rebels' behaviour before the meeting at Mile End to show why the government was afraid of them.

3 (a) Why did Richard choose Smithfield as the place for his third meeting with the rebels?

(b) Give two or more reasons why the peasants obeyed Richard after Wat Tyler was killed.

▼ *The rebels meet the King*

Meeting place	Rebel demands
	Asked to talk to King Richard. Later, sent message demanding the death of John of Gaunt and fifteen officials.
Mile End	
	Changes in the system of law. Church lands to be given to the people. All bishops, except one, to be abolished.

The effects of the Revolt

As soon as the peasants were safely back home the King's Council broke all the promises Richard had made. Many peasants were hanged for their part in the Revolt, and the villeins were not freed.

But in the long run the Revolt did help the peasants. The government never again dared to try to levy a poll tax, and lords of the manor were careful not to make their villeins work too hard or pay too much, in case they might rebel again. Often it was easier to give the villeins their freedom, rent out the land and employ labourers to do the work on the demesne. Within a century there were no villeins left in England.

Further work

1 Copy the family tree of Richard II opposite.
(a) What relation was Richard to (i) John of Gaunt, (ii) Edward III?
(b) When Richard was deposed, his cousin became King. (i) What was the new King's name? (ii) Who was his father?
(c) John of Gaunt was both rich and powerful. (i) Give an example of his wealth, and (ii) explain why he became even more powerful after his brother, Edward the Black Prince, died.

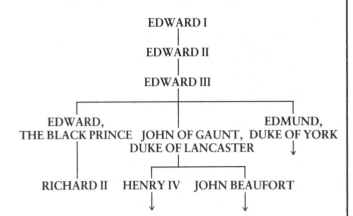

```
                    EDWARD I
                        |
                    EDWARD II
                        |
                    EDWARD III
        _____|_____
       |                |                |
    EDWARD,      JOHN OF GAUNT,      EDMUND,
 THE BLACK PRINCE DUKE OF LANCASTER  DUKE OF YORK
       |          _____|_____          ↓
       |         |            |
   RICHARD II  HENRY IV  JOHN BEAUFORT
       ↓                      ↓
```

2 Below is a family tree showing two generations of an imaginary peasant family.

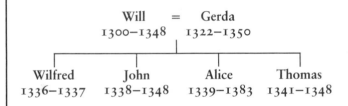

```
              Will      =      Gerda
           1300–1348        1322–1350
        _____|_____
       |         |          |            |
    Wilfred    John       Alice       Thomas
  1336–1337  1338–1348  1339–1383  1341–1348
```

(a) (i) Copy the family tree. (ii) Add a third generation to the family.
(b) (i) Why may so many members of the family have died in 1348? (ii) Who was the only member of the family to live through both the Black Death and the Peasants' Revolt?

3 (a) Make up a family tree to cover three generations of a family descended from a gentleman who was born in 1320.
(b) Which people in the family lived when (i) rents were high and labour was cheap, (ii) rents were comparatively low and wages were comparatively high?
(c) Describe how a member of the family tried to enforce *either* the Statute of Labourers, 1351, *or* the collection of the Poll Tax in 1381, and what happened as a result.

Drawing

1 Study the picture of people in Tournai churchyard on page 42.
(a) Draw one or more pictures to show how people behaved at the time of the Black Death.
(b) Write a sentence under each picture, explaining what is happening.

2 Study the picture of the peasants on the march on page 49.
(a) Why may the fourteenth-century artist have made the peasants look like soldiers?
(b) Draw a picture of the peasants marching on London, dressed in the clothes that they probably wore.

3 Study the picture of King Richard at Smithfield on page 51. It was the custom in the fourteenth century to tell a story in pictures in this way. Today, an artist would draw two pictures in a strip cartoon. Choose two incidents in the Peasants' Revolt that the same person could have taken part in, for example

John Ball preaching outside a church,
John Ball leading the peasants to London.

Draw a picture showing both these incidents, as a fourteenth-century artist might have drawn it.

→

Drama and oral work

In groups of five, prepare a reading with sound effects of the meeting at Smithfield.

1 Divide your group into three readers and two people who will produce the sound effects.
2 Take fifteen minutes to prepare your work.
3 Choose two groups to perform in front of the class.

In groups of five, prepare a mime, lasting one minute, to illustrate an aspect of life in the fourteenth century—for example, a smith at work in his forge and the peasants who come to see him because they want tools made or mended.

Rules for miming:

You must not speak,

Make your meaning clear by using bold movements,

Never really hit anyone or anything when you are miming a fight.

Quiz

1 *True or false?*
   Between 1066 and 1300 the population of England doubled.

Richard II was the nephew of John of Gaunt.

As a result of the Peasants' Revolt, all the villeins were freed immediately.

2 Make up your own 'True or false?' quiz. Write your statement followed by (true) or (false) on a piece of paper and give it in to the person in charge. Divide into two teams and hold the quiz.

Glossary

Add these words to your glossary and explain what each of them means:

tenant   statute   arable

Choose three or more words from this chapter and add them to your glossary.

Library work

In the Reference Section of your library, find a topic book on *Surnames* or look up surnames under the letter S in an encyclopedia.

1 Why did people begin to use surnames in the thirteenth century?
2 What jobs did the people who used these surnames do?

Cooper   Scrivener   Mercer

3 King and Church
The English Reformation

King Henry wants an heir

It was 1527. Henry VIII, the King of England, was worried and angry. After eighteen years of marriage he had no son to succeed him. He had a daughter, Mary, but he took it for granted that she would never be capable of ruling the country. He thought that only a man could do the job. And his wife, Catherine of Aragon, was too old to have any more children. So Henry decided that, though she had never done anything to upset him, he would divorce her and marry a younger woman who would bear him a son.

It was difficult to get a divorce in the sixteenth century. Somehow Henry had to persuade the Pope that his marriage with Catherine was against church law. Henry was sure that it was. He said that if God approved of their marriage he would have given them a son.

Catherine did not want a divorce. She believed that she and Henry were properly married. 'I take God to witness,' she told Henry, 'that I have always been to you a true and loyal wife. If there be any offence which can be alleged against me, I consent to depart. If not, then I pray you do me justice.' But Henry would not listen. He had made up his mind to divorce her.

Henry appeals to the Pope

Henry believed that the Pope was bound to be on his side. Years before, when a German monk named Martin Luther had defied the Pope, Henry had written a pamphlet contradicting him. The Pope was so pleased that he had granted Henry the title 'Defender of the Faith', which English monarchs have held ever since. So when the King's Lord Chancellor, Cardinal Wolsey, sent messengers to Rome to ask the Pope, Clement VII, to grant Henry his divorce, the King thought they would have no problem. He had already chosen a young woman named Ann Boleyn to be his next wife.

It was not as easy as he hoped. When the messengers reached Rome they found the city occupied by an army commanded by Queen Catherine's nephew, Charles V, the ruler of most of Germany. Charles did not want Pope Clement to give Henry his divorce.

Clement did not know what to do. He did not dare offend Charles V, but he did not want to upset Henry either. So he tried to delay his decision. This annoyed Henry. He thought Wolsey was not trying hard enough, so he dismissed him and turned to other people for advice.

▲ Henry VIII ruled England for thirty-eight years

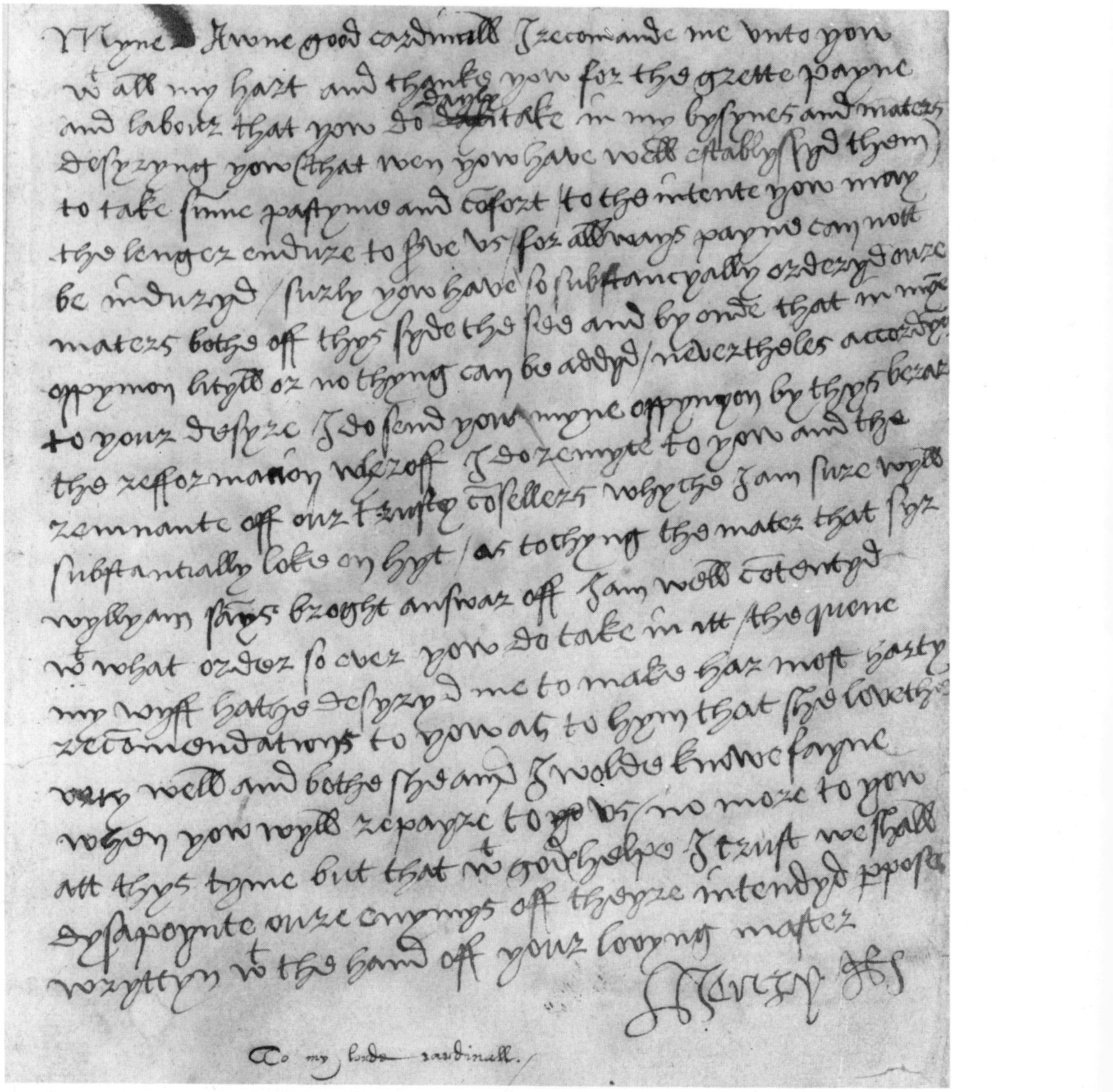

Myne awne good cardinall I recomande me unto yow
wt all my hart and thanke yow for the grette payne
and labour that yow do dayly take in my bysynes and maters
desyryng yow (that wen yow have well establyshyd them)
to take summe pastyme and comfort / to the intente yow may
the lenger endure to serve us / for allways payne can nott
be induryd / surly yow have so substancyally orderyd oure
maters bothe off thys syde the see and byonde that in myne
oppynion lyttyll or no thyng can be addyd / nevertheles accordyng
to your desyre I do send yow myne oppynyon by thys berar
the reformation wheroff I remytte to yow and the
remnante off our trusty consellers whyche I am sure wyll
substancially loke on hyt / as tochyng the mater that syr
wyllyam sandys broght answar off I am well contentyd
wt what order so ever yow do take in itt / the quene
my wyff hathe desyryd me to make har most harty
recomendations to yow as to hym that she lovethe
very well and bothe she and I wolde knowe fayne
when yow wyll repayre to us / no more to yow
att thys tyme but that wt gods helpe I trust we shall
dyssapoynte oure enymys off theyre intendyd purpose
wrytten wt the hand off your lovyng master
Henry R

To my lorde cardinall.

▲ In this letter, written in 1518, Henry VIII thanks Wolsey for his 'grette payne and labour' in his work for the King. Henry left all the boring work for Wolsey to do

The advice of Thomas Cromwell

Four years later, at the beginning of 1532, Henry was still no further forward. Wolsey had died in disgrace in 1530, but none of Henry's other advisers had been able to persuade the Pope to grant the divorce. Henry was angry and frustrated.

At last in 1532 one of his Council, Thomas Cromwell, who had been recommended to Henry by Wolsey, gave the King the idea that he needed. He advised Henry to persuade Parliament to pass an Act stating that the King, not the Pope, was head of the Church in England. Henry could then order the Archbishop of Canterbury, Thomas Cranmer, to give him his divorce.

Henry becomes head of the Church

Henry liked this scheme very much. He knew that the Members of Parliament would do as they were told. He liked the thought of being head of the English Church, and he believed that the Pope deserved to lose his power in England for treating him so badly. So he ordered Cromwell to go ahead. Within a few months Parliament passed the necessary Acts, and in May 1533 Archbishop Cranmer declared Henry's marriage to Catherine null and void.

Catherine refused to attend any of the court hearings. She still insisted that she was Henry's lawful wife and the rightful Queen of England. But Henry had already secretly married Ann Boleyn, and she was pregnant.

The birth of Elizabeth
Henry, Ann, and the whole court waited anxiously as the months passed. They all prayed for a son. At last, in September, the Queen gave birth. It was a daughter. Ann was disappointed. Henry was furious. When the baby was christened he refused to attend the service. She was named Elizabeth, after Henry's mother.

Henry's anger soon passed. Queen Ann was still young, and there was plenty of time for her to bear the son he longed for.

▶ This is the most famous portrait of Ann Boleyn. She was only twenty-nine when she was executed

Studying the story

How do we know?

Catherine's letters
In 1531 Henry refused to live with Catherine any longer and sent her away from his court. For the next five years, until she died in 1536, Catherine moved from one country house to another, with only a few ladies-in-waiting to keep her company.

While Henry's lawyers were trying to persuade the Pope that Henry and Catherine were never legally married, Catherine wrote to the Pope and Charles V putting her point of view. She gave these letters to Eustache de Chapuys, one of the few people allowed to visit her. Chapuys was Charles's ambassador or representative in England, and he was the only person Catherine trusted to deliver her letters safely.

Henry never came to see her, so Catherine also had to write to him. Many of her letters to the King were about their daughter, Mary, who was not allowed to see her mother. In 1535 Catherine was worried because she had heard that Mary was very ill. Chapuys suspected that Mary was being poisoned and Catherine wrote this letter to him, asking for his help:

'My special friend: My physician has told me something of my daughter's illness . . . I beg you to speak to the King, and desire him . . . to send his daughter and mine to where I am . . . say to his Highness that there is no need for anyone to nurse her but myself, that I will put her in my own bed in my own chamber and watch her when needful.'

Henry would not let Mary go to her mother, but he did give permission to Catherine's doctor to visit the princess.

▼ How Catherine used Chapuys to carry her letters

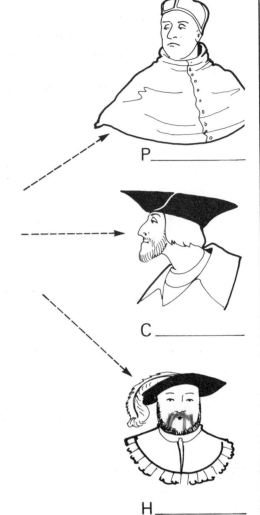

P_____

Letters and messages

C_____

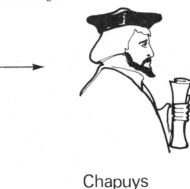

Chapuys

C_____

H_____

Copy and complete the diagram.

1 Why did Catherine
   (a) Write letters to Henry after 1531, instead of talking to him,
   (b) Write to the Pope and Charles V while the lawyers were arguing about the divorce case?

2 Who was Eustache de Chapuys and why did Catherine give him the letters that she wrote?

3 (a) What did Catherine ask Chapuys to do for her in 1535?
   (b) Do her letters seem to have had little or much influence on Henry by 1535? Give reasons for your answer.

What do you think?
Charles V relied on Chapuys to keep him informed about events in England. Would Chapuys' information about Henry and Catherine have been reliable? Give reasons for your answer.

The legal documents
We still have many of the legal documents to do with Henry and Catherine's divorce. Two of the most important ones are:

1533 The Act of Parliament saying that Henry had always been the head of the Church and the church courts in England.

1533 The written record of the court set up by the King to try the divorce case. Archbishop Cranmer was the judge.

Many important people were present in Parliament and in the court when these events took place.

1 Name the archbishop who judged the divorce case.

2 Look at the diagram of Parliament on page 11. Give two examples of the kind of people who attended Parliament when an Act was passed.

3 Copy the statement below that you think is
the more accurate:
   Many important people helped Henry to
   enforce the law of the land.
   Many important people let Henry
   change the law in order to get his own
   way.

What do you think?
A document may have been witnessed by many
important people. Does this mean that the
information in it must be true? Use the
information about the legal documents to do
with the divorce to illustrate your answer.

Understanding what happened

1 (a) Copy the time chart opposite and use
these names to fill in the spaces correctly:
   Wolsey Cromwell Henry
      Cranmer Pope Ann
(b) Who advised Henry to use Parliament to
make himself the head of the English
Church?
(c) How many years did it take Henry to get
his divorce?

What do you think?
Why did Henry go to so much trouble to make
his divorce appear to be legal?

1527	King _____ decides to divorce Catherine.
1530	_____ fails to persuade _____ Clement to give Henry a divorce and dies in disgrace.
1532	Thomas _____ advises Henry to use Parliament to make himself head of the English Church.
1533	Parliament does as Henry wishes, and he is made head of the English Church. The new Archbishop of Canterbury, _____, grants Henry a divorce. Henry marries _____ Boleyn and Elizabeth is born.

2 (a) Copy the family tree below and fill in the
gaps.

```
CATHERINE = HENRY = ANN BOLEYN
OF ARAGON            (married _____)
(married 1509)

        _____  ELIZABETH
       (born 1516) (born _____)
```

(b) For how many years was Catherine
married to Henry before he divorced her?
(c) How old was Mary when Elizabeth was
born?

What do you think?
Why was Henry so angry when Elizabeth was
born?
3 (a) Why did Henry think that the Pope
would grant him his divorce?
(b) Why was Charles V able to stop the Pope
granting the divorce?
(c) How did Catherine show that she
thought Archbishop Cranmer's court was
illegal?

What do you think?
Why was the King of England more powerful in
1533 than he was in 1527?

Further work

Writing

1 Write the letter that Chapuys might have sent to Charles V in 1535, telling him that Mary was ill and saying what her father and mother were doing about it.

2 Write the letter that Wolsey might have sent to Rome in 1527, asking the Pope to grant Henry a divorce and reminding him that Henry was one of his supporters.

3 In 1533 Henry wrote to Catherine, telling her to send him the robe in which Mary was christened. Catherine refused to part with the robe.

(a) Write the letter that Henry might have written to Catherine, explaining why he wanted the robe.

(b) Write Catherine's reply, giving her reasons for refusing to part with the robe.

Drawing

1 (a) Draw the picture of Hampton Court.

(b) Why did Wolsey build Hampton Court?

(c) Why did Henry dismiss Wolsey and take Hampton Court away from him?

2 Chapuys wrote to Charles V saying that when Henry heard that Catherine was dead he dressed from head to foot in yellow and held a dance to celebrate the good news. Look at the picture of Henry on page 55.

(a) Draw a picture of Henry celebrating the news of Catherine's death.

(b) Write a sentence saying how we know that Henry behaved in this way.

3 (a) Draw a picture for each of these captions:

Henry sends Catherine away.

Catherine writes letters from her home in the country.

Catherine walks out of Cranmer's court.

Catherine dictates her last letter.

(b) Write a title for your set of pictures.

Discussion

1 (a) Write down two or three reasons why you agree or disagree with each of the following statements about Henry VIII:

He treated his first wife and daughter harshly.

He chose his government officials wisely.

He tried to safeguard England's future.

(b) Choose two people to read out their answers. Do the rest of you agree or disagree with them? Give reasons for your opinions.

(c) At the end of your discussion see how many of you agree or disagree with this statement:

Henry was a very selfish man.

For your glossary

Explain in your own words:

ambassador   null and void

◀ The gateway of Hampton Court Palace as it looks today. Hampton Court was built by Cardinal Wolsey as a country home. Henry took it from him in 1529. During the next ten years Henry improved and enlarged it. Today the palace and gardens are visited by thousands of people every year

The Wars of the Roses

English Kings in the fifteenth century

Henry VIII was the richest king to rule England for more than 100 years. For most of the fifteenth century, Kings of England had little wealth or power. First they wasted their treasure fighting the Hundred Years War against France. Then a civil war broke out in England between the Yorkists and the Lancastrians, two branches of the royal family, over which of them had a better right to rule the country.

While the civil war was going on landowners often took the law into their own hands. For example, in about 1458 Margaret Paston, who lived in Norfolk, wrote to her husband, Sir John, who was away from home on business. She asked him to bring back some crossbows and a supply of arrows. Sir John had quarrelled with the servants of an important landowner who lived in the area. Margaret was afraid that they might attack her home, and she wanted to be able to fight back.

The war ended in 1485 when Henry Tudor, a Lancastrian, defeated the Yorkists, and became King Henry VII. He kept the country at peace, enforced law and order, and saved money. When he died in 1509 he left his son, Henry VIII, a full treasury.

▼ The rulers of England, 1399–1547

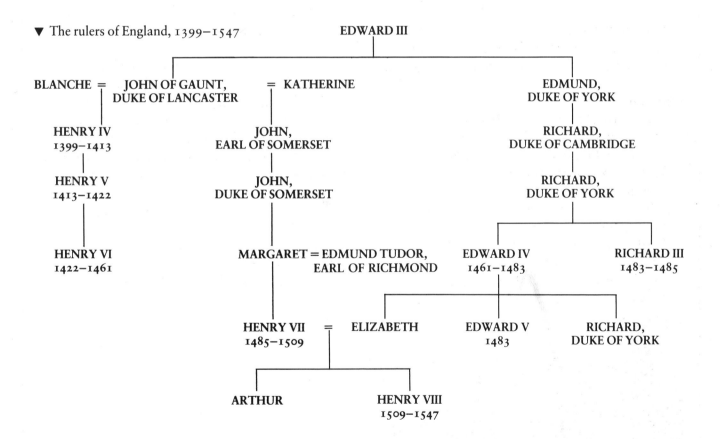

EDWARD III

BLANCHE = JOHN OF GAUNT, DUKE OF LANCASTER = KATHERINE

EDMUND, DUKE OF YORK

HENRY IV 1399–1413

JOHN, EARL OF SOMERSET

RICHARD, DUKE OF CAMBRIDGE

HENRY V 1413–1422

JOHN, DUKE OF SOMERSET

RICHARD, DUKE OF YORK

HENRY VI 1422–1461

MARGARET = EDMUND TUDOR, EARL OF RICHMOND

EDWARD IV 1461–1483

RICHARD III 1483–1485

HENRY VII 1485–1509 = ELIZABETH

EDWARD V 1483

RICHARD, DUKE OF YORK

ARTHUR

HENRY VIII 1509–1547

The Yorkists' emblem was a white rose. The Lancastrians' emblem was a red rose. The Tudor rose joined the white and red roses together

The Roses

1 (a) Give two reasons why the kings who ruled England in the fifteenth century had little wealth or power.

(b) Who became King of England in 1485?

(c) What did he do that made his son the richest King of England for more than a hundred years?

2 (a) What do we think was the date of the letter that Margaret Paston wrote to her husband?

(b) Who was the King of England at that time?

(c) Judging from the letter, was the King able to enforce law and order in Norfolk? Give reasons for your answer.

3 (a) What was the name of the princess whom Henry VII married in 1485?

(b) Henry thought that it would help to keep the peace if he married this princess. Explain why.

(c) Henry VIII thought that England was more likely to remain at peace if he had a son. What reason or reasons may he have had to think this?

OUT OF 20

Bluff King Hal

Henry VIII enjoyed being King. He liked to be admired and waited on, and liked the pomp and splendour of the court. He was fit and active, and loved hunting, fighting in tournaments and playing tennis. Henry was also very well educated. He spoke French and Latin, understood mathematics and astronomy, and was famous for his knowledge of religion. He could play several musical instruments, sang well, and wrote a great deal of music.

Henry could be charming and affectionate, but there was another side to his character. He was impatient, and had no time for everyday business. He was obstinate and suspicious. Henry once said, 'If I thought my cap knew my thoughts, I would throw it into the fire.'

But above all, Henry was arrogant and selfish. He would sacrifice anybody if he thought he could gain by it. Thomas More, a good friend, said, 'If my head would win him a castle in France, it should not fail to go.'

The King and the Church

Henry did not want to share power with anyone. He thought that he had the right to control every aspect of life in England,

▲ Thomas More wrote several books, and was famous all over Europe for his learning

including the Church. Most people did not realise how strongly Henry felt. They did not take his claim to be head of the Church seriously. Kings and Popes had often quarrelled, but had always agreed in the end. People took it for granted that this would happen again.

A few of Henry's advisers knew better. They realised that the King would never give up his claim, and they suspected that he would take land and money from the Church, and order the bishops and clergy to do as he wished.

The deaths of Fisher and More

Sir Thomas More, who was Lord Chancellor, and John Fisher, Bishop of Rochester, both disagreed with Henry's claim to be head of the Church. So More resigned, and Fisher said that in his opinion, the Pope was still the rightful head of the Church, whatever Parliament had said. This was a very dangerous statement—in fact Parliament had just passed an Act that made it treason.

Fisher was old and ill, but when Henry heard what he had said he ordered him to be arrested and charged with treason. The new Pope, Paul III, heard of his arrest, and made Fisher a cardinal, thinking that Henry would not dare harm him. But the King was not impressed. Fisher was found guilty, and beheaded on 22 June 1535.

Henry was also determined to get rid of More. But Sir Thomas was a trained lawyer, so when asked if he thought the King was the rightful head of the Church, he refused to commit himself. In the end the Solicitor-General, Richard Rich, was ordered to swear he had heard More say that Parliament had not got the power to make the King head of the Church. Rich was lying, but More was found guilty of treason and beheaded on 6 July 1535. He said he died 'as the King's good servant, but God's first'.

Fisher and More were Henry's most famous victims, but altogether he had about 45 people killed. Most were monks, who refused to accept the King as head of the Church. They were treated with appalling cruelty. Three were kept standing for more than a fortnight, held upright by iron collars chained to the wall, while their legs and arms were weighed down with chains. Some monks died in prison. The rest were hanged, drawn and quartered.

Study

Henry and his victims

A monk

4

Bishop of Rochester

Said Parliament could not make Henry the head of the Church

Beheaded, even though the Pope made him a cardinal

King Henry

2

John Fisher

2

Parliament made him head of the English Church

Quarrelled with the Pope

Declared that men who supported the Pope were traitors

Thomas More

4

1 (a) Divide a double page into four sections and draw one of the heads above in each section. Leave enough space under each of your drawings for notes.

(b) The descriptions fit two of the people whose heads you have drawn. Write the descriptions in the correct sections of your diagram.

(c) Write three important points about each of the other two people whose heads you have drawn.

What do you think?

Many people in England agreed with the men who were executed. Why were there no protests against the executions?

OUT OF 15   × 1.833333

64

The monks lose their power

Monasteries and education

At the beginning of the sixteenth century monasteries played an important part in the life of the country. For instance, most schools were run by monks or nuns. Nuns taught girls to read, sing and embroider, while boys were taught by monks in grammar schools. The boys spent most of their time learning Latin. This was necessary because scholars all over Europe understood Latin. They wrote all their books, including school textbooks, in Latin, and when they met they spoke to each other in Latin.

Most children did not go to school, but the rich sent their sons and daughters to be educated, and they grew up to respect the monks and nuns who had taught them. But by 1530 the situation had changed.

St Paul's School and the New Learning

Some of the Latin textbooks used by the monks were translations of works written by Greek scholars hundreds of years before the birth of Christ. During the fifteenth century, scholars who understood Greek examined copies of the original Greek manuscripts, and compared them with the Latin translations in the textbooks. They found many mistakes in the books, so that people who relied on them could have no idea of what the Greeks had taught. The scholars who studied the Greek manuscripts felt that they were able to look at the world in a completely new way. So they called their Greek studies the New Learning.

One of these scholars was John Colet, Dean of St Paul's Cathedral, and a friend of Sir Thomas More. He thought boys ought to be taught to understand this new learning, so in 1509 he opened a school for 150 boys in the Cathedral grounds. St Paul's differed from other schools in two ways. The boys had to learn Greek as well as Latin, and their teachers were married men, not monks.

Pupils had to work hard at St Paul's. Lessons began at 7 a.m. Each boy had to arrive on time carrying a satchel containing his textbooks, a Latin Bible, a quill pen, paper and ink. In winter the boys had to bring candles to read by.

In the middle of the day they all went home for two hours for something to eat, and then they worked again until 5 p.m., when lessons finished.

Scholars who had been to St Paul's were proud of their school. They thought that traditional schools run by monks and nuns were out of date, and they had no respect for them.

Erasmus and the New Testament

Erasmus was a Dutch scholar, and a friend of More and Colet. He did not like the Latin version of the Bible used by the Church. He found a Greek version of the New Testament written by some of the first Christians, and published it. He also translated it into Latin. His version was different from that used by the Church, and Erasmus claimed it was more accurate. Some monks disagreed. They said that Erasmus had changed the meaning of some of the things Jesus had said.

Erasmus believed that the Bible ought to be translated into every language, so that everybody could read and understand it. In Germany, Martin Luther agreed with Erasmus, and he translated the Bible into German, using Erasmus's New Testament to help him. Most churchmen thought that ordinary people ought not to be allowed to read the Bible in case they misunderstood it.

Erasmus and the monks

When he was a boy Erasmus had been sent to train as a monk, but he hated the life, and had left the monastery. In 1509 he wrote a book called *The Praise of Folly*. In it he made fun of monks. He said that they were ignorant and self-satisfied, and he accused them of 'filling boys' heads with arrant nonsense' instead of educating them properly. *The Praise of Folly* was very popular. Educated people read and discussed it, and laughed at Erasmus's description of monks 'braying like donkeys during their services', and 'bellowing for bread from door to door'.

By 1530 many educated people had lost their respect for monks and monasteries.

Read and remember

Paper was very expensive, so the boys who went to St Paul's School could not write down everything they had to remember. Instead, they had to learn their work thoroughly and were tested by their teachers.

1 Learn the sections headed 'St Paul's School and the New Learning' and 'Erasmus and the New Testament'. Do not try to learn every word, but read both sections twice.

2 Make sure you know:

The names of the men mentioned and what each of them did.

How St Paul's was different from most schools and what happened during the school day.

Why scholars learnt Greek as well as Latin and called their studies the 'New Learning'.

3 Close your books and make up three questions about the work you have learnt. Write each question on a separate piece of paper, give them in to your teacher and hold a quiz.

4 Write about one of the following without looking at any notes:

Dean Colet and St Paul's School,

Erasmus,

Luther and the New Testament,

The New Learning.

Thomas Cromwell and the monasteries

The wealth of the monasteries

As head of the Church Henry was in control of England's monasteries. They were very rich. Monasteries owned about a quarter of all the land in England, and had a total income of about £200,000 a year. This was nearly double what Henry himself had at the beginning of his reign.

By 1534 the King was very short of money. He was always extravagant. He loved jewels, and fine clothing and palaces. He quarrelled with other rulers and plunged the country into war. This was expensive. Henry had to buy ships and weapons, pay troops, and keep them supplied with gunpowder, cannon balls, arrows, wagons, horses, food and fodder for their animals. It could cost £100,000 a year to keep an army in the field, and by 1534 the King's treasury was empty.

The monasteries and the people

In order to fill the royal treasury Henry and his new minister, Thomas Cromwell, decided to take land and money from the monasteries. Recently fewer people than before had become monks and nuns, and many monasteries were half empty. In some, the monks led very comfortable lives, eating more and praying less than they ought to. This made them unpopular.

But there were still many monasteries where men lived simple, holy lives. People respected them. Monasteries were also useful to travellers, who stayed overnight on their journeys. Beggars visited them for gifts of food and money. The old and sick went to them for help, and country gentlemen still sent their sons and daughters to the monks and nuns to be educated.

▲ A groat, or fourpenny piece, minted during Henry VIII's reign. He and his father, Henry VII, were the first English Kings to have their portraits on coins

▼ Peterborough Abbey Church is now used as the cathedral. The eastern chapels were built in about 1500

Henry and Cromwell wanted to seize all the wealth of the monasteries, but they knew that if they suddenly took such a big step they would frighten and upset people all over the country. So they went to work slowly and carefully.

The visitation

As a first step Cromwell sent inspectors known as visitors to the monasteries. The visitors had to find out if the monasteries had anything of value, how many monks there were, and if they were obeying the rules of their order.

Cromwell divided the country into districts. Each visitor was given a district, and inspected all the monasteries in it. The visitors set out in the rainy summer of 1535. They got soaked as they rode along the green lanes to the monasteries, where bells rang regularly, calling monks to pray. The monks knew that visitors were coming, but they were not alarmed. Such inspections were quite common.

The visitors were in a hurry. Each of them had many monasteries to inspect. So as a rule they stayed only a few hours at each. They questioned the abbot and his monks, told them to be loyal to the King, and instructed them to keep the rules of their order. Then they left the monastery to write their report and move on to the next.

The visitors' reports

The visitors knew that Henry and Cromwell wanted them to show up the faults of the monasteries, so as a rule their reports were critical. The visitor to the monastery at Bury St Edmunds in Suffolk wrote:

> 'As for the abbot ... it was detected that ... he delighted much in playing dice and cards, and therein spent much money ... It was confessed and proved that there [were] women coming and resorting to this monastery ... Amongst the relics we found much vanity and superstition, as the coals that St Laurence was roasted with, the parings of St Edmund's nails, St Thomas of Canterbury's penknife and his boots.'

At Landon Abbey, near Dover, the visitor described the abbot as 'the drunkenest knave living' and his monks 'as bad as he, without a spark of virtue'.

Even where they could find nothing wrong the visitors did not praise the monks. Richard Leyton visited Glastonbury where the monks were famous for their piety. He wrote that they were 'so straight kept that they cannot offend: but fain they would if they might'.

The dissolution of the monasteries begins

The visitors' reports showed up the monasteries in a bad light, and they gave Henry the excuse he needed to close some of them down and take their lands. To be on the safe side he started with the smaller, less important ones which had fewest friends. In spring 1536, Parliament passed an Act closing all monasteries with an income of less than £200 a year. Commissioners were to visit them and make a thorough survey of all they possessed. Then the monasteries were to be closed, and the monks sent away. A special court was set up to administer all the monastic land.

Study

Money and the monasteries

1 (a) Read the sections on the wealth of the monasteries, and the monasteries and the people, on page 66.

(b) Copy the diagram below and fill in the spaces correctly.

(c) Copy the picture of the groat of Henry VIII on page 66 into the circle.

How Henry used his income

In peacetime
Income a year: £_____.
Paid government officials.
Bought jewels, palaces,
fine clothes.

In wartime
Cost of paying an army:
£_____.
Bought ships
and weapons.
Paid _____ and _____.
Provided supplies, e.g.
_____ and _____.

To raise more money
Thomas _____
and Henry wanted
to confiscate the
_____ of
the monasteries.

ACID

How the monks used their income

Total income a year
of all monasteries:
£_____. Provided:
lodgings for _____,
gifts of _____ and
_____ to beggars,
help for the _____
and _____, schools
for the _____
of gentlemen.

*Some had more money
than they needed*
Some monasteries were half
_____ and the monks were
able to spend money making
themselves comfortable.

Visitors at Bury St Edmunds

A relic was something connected with a dead saint—for example: a splinter of bone from a skull, or a piece of clothing that he or she was said to have worn. The relic was kept in a shrine in a monastery. Pilgrims who wanted to ask for a blessing, or who were crippled or ill, came to the monastery. They knelt in front of the shrine and asked the saint to pray to God for them.

1 List three relics that the visitors found at the monastery at Bury St Edmunds.

2 St Edmund was killed by the Danes in 870. How likely is it that the relics that the monks claimed to be his were genuine? Give reasons for your answer.

3 Monks made three vows:
 to be poor all their lives,
 never to marry or live with women,
 to obey their abbot.

(a) The visitor to Bury St Edmunds said the abbot and monks there had broken two of their vows. Which were they?

(b) Quote the words from the report which accuse the monks of breaking their vows.

Unrest and rebellion

Unrest at court

There were also important events at court in 1536. In January Queen Catherine died, and Henry had a serious accident. He fell heavily from his horse and lay unconscious for two hours. Queen Ann was pregnant at the time, and was so upset that she had a miscarriage.

Henry was disappointed. He was already tired of Ann, and was flirting with one of her ladies-in-waiting named Jane Seymour. Now he thought that Ann would never have a son, and he wanted to get rid of her and marry Jane. So at the beginning of May, Ann was arrested and accused of having had love affairs with five

◀ A sixteenth-century painting of Henry VIII with his Parliament. Before the dissolution of the monasteries, the abbots of some of the richest abbeys sat in Parliament with the bishops on the King's right. The Speaker of the House of Commons stands respectfully opposite the King, waiting for instructions

men, including her own brother, since she had married Henry.

Ann denied the charge, but was sent to the Tower. She told the lieutenant, 'I shall die without justice.' He said that even if she was the poorest subject in the realm she would have justice. Ann laughed. She knew Henry better.

The five men were also arrested. Four denied the charge, but one, Mark Smeaton, a court musician, confessed. He was probably tortured. Ann and the five men were all tried, all found guilty and sentenced to death. On 19 May, Ann was beheaded. On the same day Henry appeared at court in very good spirits, and on 20 May he and Jane Seymour were married. In October 1537 Jane gave birth to a boy, but she died soon after. Though Henry lost his Queen, he had the son he had been longing for. The boy was christened Edward. He seemed healthy, and in the rejoicing at his birth the death of his mother passed almost unnoticed.

In 1540 Henry married Anne of Cleves, a Dutch princess. He found he disliked her, so he got a divorce. He then married Catherine Howard, niece of the Duke of Norfolk. He discovered that she was having love affairs with two courtiers, so he had her executed. Finally he married Catherine Parr, a widow, who outlived him.

Revolt in Lincolnshire
In the autumn of 1536 the commissioners were

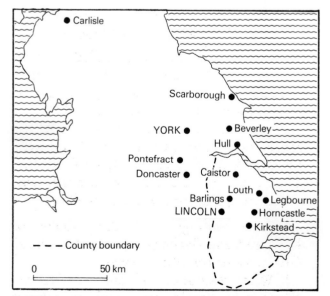

▲ Northern England, showing Lincolnshire at the time of the Revolt

at work closing down the smaller monasteries, and Henry was celebrating his marriage to Jane with feasts, concerts and pageants. Suddenly a rebellion broke out in Lincolnshire.

The county had been unsettled for some time. There were three sets of government commissioners at work there. Some were collecting taxes, some were closing down monasteries. Others were questioning the ordinary parish priests to make sure that they were learned and decent, and fit to do their jobs.

All these agents at work made people uneasy, and the county was full of rumours. Some said that the King planned to impose taxes on everyday items such as white bread, pigs and geese. Others said that Henry wanted to close half the churches in the country, and take all their silver plate and jewels for himself. As a rule nobody would have believed such stories, but now they were not so sure. A king who dared to close down the monasteries might do anything.

The revolt in Lincolnshire started on 1 October in Louth. The vicar told his congregation that commissioners were due there the next day to question him. The congregation decided to send them packing. Under the command of a shoemaker, Nicholas Melton, who called himself Captain Cobbler, they collected axes, swords, sticks and pitchforks, and mounted guard on their church. When the commissioners arrived the mob seized them, burnt their books and papers, and made them swear an oath to support the common people. Clergy came from nearby parishes, expecting to meet the commissioners, and Captain Cobbler sent the priests home to tell their congregations to join in a march on Lincoln.

The revolt spreads
Soon there were several hundred rebels. Some went to a convent at Legbourne and drove away the commissioners who were closing it down. Others went to Kirkstead Abbey, demanded food and money, and insisted that the monks joined them. When the abbot refused they threatened to burn down the abbey. In the end the monks marched off with them, but later gave them the slip and went back to Kirkstead.

Later, some rebels reached Barlings, a small

abbey east of Lincoln. They demanded food and shelter. The abbot fed them, and let them sleep in the barn. The next day the rebels asked the monks to join them. At first they refused, but the rebels swore at them and threatened to destroy the abbey. They left with six of the strongest monks, six bullocks, beer, bread and cheese.

There were also riots in Caistor and Horncastle. A government commissioner and the Bishop of Lincoln's chief clerk were killed. Then some local landowners, led by Lord Hussey, once a staunch supporter of Queen Catherine, took charge. They drew up a number of demands to be presented to the King. They wanted Henry to abolish all taxes in peacetime, reopen the monasteries, and dismiss and punish his new advisers, such as Rich and Cromwell.

The revolt is crushed

When Henry heard of the revolt, he described Lincolnshire as 'one of the most brute and beastly shires of the whole realm'. He said that the rebels were 'false traitors' and sent his brother-in-law, the Duke of Suffolk, with about 5,000 troops to suppress the rebellion. He ordered Suffolk to 'burn and kill man, woman and child, to the terrible example of all others'.

Suffolk was a sensible man. He issued a proclamation assuring the rebels that Henry would not close any churches, and threatening them with merciless slaughter if they did not surrender. The leaders gave in, and by 18 October all the rebels had gone home. On 14 November everyone except for 140 men who were in prison received a royal pardon. The revolt was over.

Study

Rebels in Lincolnshire, 1536

Draw the outline of the map of northern England on page 70 and shade in Lincolnshire.

1 (a) List the events below in the order in which they happened:

A mob drives the King's commissioners away from Louth Church.

Lord Hussey joins the rebels and sends their demands to the King.

Rebels roam Lincolnshire, trying to gain support from the monks.

Three sets of government commissioners go to Lincolnshire.

Riots break out and a commissioner is killed.

(b) Add two more important events to your list, showing how Henry and Suffolk behaved during the rebellion.

(c) Copy the statement which you think is the more accurate:

Most of the rebels were pardoned.

Most of the rebels were executed.

2 (a) Make a list showing what each of the government commissions was doing in Lincolnshire.

(b) List three examples of the rumours that were going around Lincolnshire.

(c) List the three demands the rebels sent to Henry.

3 (a) Copy out the sentences below using the correct names to fill in the gaps:

King Henry   the Duke of Suffolk
Nicholas Melton   Lord Hussey

_____ _____, who called himself Captain Cobbler, led the rebellion at Louth.
_____ _____, who had supported Queen Catherine, sided with the rebels.
_____ _____ gave orders that the rebels and their wives and children were to be burnt and killed as an example to others.
The _____ __ _____ went north with 5,000 troops to suppress the rebellion.

(b) How willingly did the monks of Kirkstead and Barlings support the rebels? Give reasons for your answer.

(c) What assurance did Suffolk give the rebels in his proclamation and what threat did he make?

The Pilgrimage of Grace

In October 1536 a rebellion broke out in Yorkshire. Sir Robert Aske, a lawyer, led the people of east Yorkshire on what he called a 'Pilgrimage of Grace' to try to persuade the King to dismiss his ministers, restore the monasteries and recognise the Pope as head of the Church. His men carried banners and wore badges showing the five wounds of Christ.

On 16 October Aske captured York. On 21 October the commander of Pontefract Castle, Lord Darcy, surrendered to Aske and joined the pilgrimage. Before the end of October the rebels controlled almost the whole of England north of Cheshire and Lincolnshire.

Henry sends Norfolk to crush the revolt

Henry had no intention of giving way to the rebels. Instead he sent his most experienced general, the Duke of Norfolk, to crush the rebellion. But Norfolk had only 8,000 men, and when he reached Doncaster on his way north he found his way blocked by an army of 30,000 men commanded by Aske, Darcy and Sir Robert Constable, a local landowner. Many of the rebels were from noble families. Norfolk described their army as 'the flower of the north'.

Norfolk knew that if he attacked the rebels he would be defeated, and they would be able to advance south and perhaps take over the whole country. So he decided to negotiate. But first he wrote to Henry: 'Sir, most humbly I beseech you to take in good part whatsoever promises I shall make unto the rebels ... for surely I shall observe no part thereof.'

On 27 October Norfolk met the rebel leaders on Doncaster Bridge, and promised that if they drew up a list of their demands he would present them to the King. He let the rebels think that he was on their side, and they felt sure that Henry would give way.

Norfolk agrees to the rebels' demands

It took the rebels more than a month to draw up a formal list of their demands, and on 6 December they met Norfolk again. As before they asked the King to reopen the monasteries he had closed, to restore the Pope's power, and to dismiss and punish Cromwell. They now also wanted Henry to call a new Parliament to meet in York. Norfolk promised that no more monasteries would be closed, and that a new Parliament would be called. But he told the rebels that he would have to take their other demands back to Henry for him to decide. He then proclaimed a royal pardon for all the rebels, and set off for London.

Aske was satisfied. He thought he had won. He took off his pilgrim's badge, and persuaded the people that their pilgrimage was at an end. The men went home, and Aske went on a visit to court, where Henry received him very kindly. Aske trusted the King, and when he returned to the north he told his friends how charming and pleasant Henry had been. But some of his men were very suspicious.

The revolt breaks out again

Aske's friends had heard rumours that Henry planned to send extra troops to garrison his castles in the north. Then he would arrest the leaders of the rebellion and put them on trial. They decided to strike first, and in January 1537 a few Yorkshire landowners attacked the castles at Hull, Beverley and Scarborough. The rebels were defeated, but the fact that fighting had begun again gave Henry the excuse he needed to cancel his pardon. He sent Norfolk back to Yorkshire to punish the rebels.

While he was in York trying to decide which rebels to hang and which to pardon, the Duke heard news that 6,000 peasants in Cumberland had rebelled and were attacking Carlisle. Henry heard the news too, and ordered Norfolk to go north and 'cause such dreadful execution upon a good number of the inhabitants, hanging them on trees, quartering them and setting the quarters in every town, as shall be a fearful warning.' Norfolk went to Cumberland with 4,000 troops, and the rebels at once

▼ Thomas Cromwell. As well as organising the dissolution of the monasteries, he set up a new system of government. Henry VIII called him 'the most faithful servant I ever had'

surrendered. He hanged 74 of them on trees in their own gardens. He apologised to Henry for hanging so few, but he felt sorry for 'the poor caitiffs' who had been very badly treated by their landlords, 'which as I and all others think, was the only cause of the rebellion'.

The rebel leaders are punished

The punishment of the Yorkshire rebels continued. Thomas Cromwell took charge of the arrangements. Most of the trials took place in Yorkshire, Durham and Lincolnshire, but the leaders were taken to London and tried in Westminster Hall. The two lords, Darcy and Hussey, were first. They were both condemned to death. When Darcy was sentenced he said, 'Cromwell, it is thou that art . . . the chief cause of all this rebellion . . . and though thou wouldst procure all the noblemen's heads within the realm to be stricken off, yet shall one remain that shall strike off thy head.' Cromwell was unmoved. Darcy and Hussey were both beheaded.

The day after Darcy's trial Aske and fifteen others were tried. They were all condemned to death. Most of them were hanged at Tyburn in London. The only woman among them was burnt at Smithfield. Sir Robert Constable was hanged at Hull, 'above the highest gate of the town', and Robert Aske was hanged at York, with all the gentry of the county summoned to watch. In all 216 rebels were executed. It was a very small proportion of the number of people who took part in the revolt.

Summing up

The Pilgrimage of Grace was one of the most dangerous rebellions in English history. At one time the pilgrims controlled nearly half the country, and if they had marched south from Doncaster instead of negotiating with Norfolk, they might well have conquered London, because the King was very unpopular. Yet the Pilgrimage was not a violent revolt. The Lincolnshire rebels killed two men, but once Aske had taken charge, nobody was harmed.

The Pilgrimage of Grace

What made the rebels join together in the Pilgrimage of Grace? Here are some of the reasons that historians have suggested.

Prices were rising

Today we expect prices to rise every year, but at the beginning of the sixteenth century people were used to them staying the same. During Henry VIII's reign the price of many goods kept on rising, year after year. People did not understand, and blamed the King's advisers.

Religion was changing

Many rebels disliked the changes that Henry had made. They wanted him to make the Pope head of the Church again, reopen the monasteries he had closed, and leave the rest alone.

Landowners had lost their influence

The important landowners were used to advising the King on how to govern the country. Many of them were friends of Queen Catherine, and when Henry divorced her they lost the influence they once had with him.

Thomas Cromwell had gained power

All the men who joined the Pilgrimage of Grace wanted the King to get rid of Cromwell. He had helped Henry to divorce Catherine, was the King's chief adviser, and he was in charge of the scheme to take over the monasteries. Once, Cromwell had been a lawyer's clerk and a common soldier, but now he was the most powerful man in England after the King.

Landlord

Tenant farmer

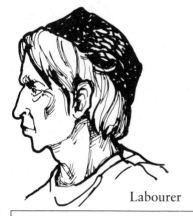

Labourer

Landlord	Tenant farmer	Labourer
Finds his standard of living falling so puts up tenants' rents. Thinks the King should listen to his advice. Thinks the King should not be head of both the Church and the government.	Finds it hard to pay higher rent and rising prices. Thinks the King does not understand problems in the north. Fears the monastery school his son attends will be closed.	Works for monks on their land. Can find no other work in this area. Relies on the monks to look after him if he becomes too ill or too old to work.

1 *In pairs*, make a list of the reasons why each of the people above may have thought that Thomas Cromwell:
   (a) had changed their lives for the worse,
   (b) would probably make their lives more difficult in the future.

2 Choose someone to read his or her answers to the class. What do the rest of you think?

3 Choose one or more of the people shown above. Write a paragraph explaining what he may have hoped to gain by joining the Pilgrimage of Grace.

What happened to the rebels?

1 (a) Using the outline map at the beginning of the book, draw the outline of England and Wales below.

(b) Fill in the names of the two towns.

(c) Copy the notes in the boxes and fill in the spaces with the correct words. Use pages 72 and 73 to help you.

(d) What is an annotated map?

2 **Discussion**

How dangerous were the rebels?

Two hundred and sixteen leaders of the Pilgrimage of Grace were condemned to death as traitors to the King. Henry had them executed as a warning to others. Did he need to make an example of them?

(a) Divide into two groups.

Group 1 In pairs, list the reasons why the rebels could have been dangerous to the King and his government. Consider:

The kind of people who led the rebellion,

The size of their army,

Any other points that you think are important.

N.B. Write key words only. For example, your first note might be:

Leaders:

Sir Robert Aske—lawyer.

Nobles, e.g. Lord Darcy.

Important people—could raise armies and vote in Parliament.

Group 2 In pairs, list the reasons why the rebels may have felt that they were trying to make a peaceful protest but were betrayed by the King. Consider:

Why they called the uprising a pilgrimage,

The demands they made to the King,

Any other points that you think are important.

N.B. Write key words only. For example, your first note might be:

Pilgrimage:

Peaceful—seeking a blessing

—trying to show they did not want violence.

(b) Choose two people, one from each group, to read out their notes. Do the rest of you agree? Give reasons for your opinions, using your notes to help you.

(c) Take a vote on whether or not you think Henry was justified in hanging the leaders of the Pilgrimage of Grace.

What do you think?

Why is it easier to hold a discussion if you have clear notes to work from?

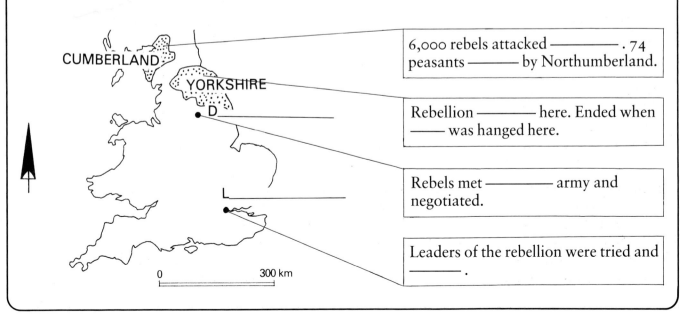

CUMBERLAND

YORKSHIRE

D_____

0   300 km

6,000 rebels attacked ———— . 74 peasants ———— by Northumberland.

Rebellion ———— here. Ended when ———— was hanged here.

Rebels met ———— army and negotiated.

Leaders of the rebellion were tried and ————— .

The end of the monasteries

The Pilgrimage of Grace had no effect on Henry's policies. He continued to close down the monasteries and take over their land. Soon he had closed all the smaller monasteries. Then he started on the larger ones. By the end of 1540, all the monasteries in England had been closed, and the special court Henry had set up was busy dealing with their possessions.

Their land and buildings

The monasteries' most valuable possession was their land. If Henry had kept it all for himself and passed it on to his children, the English royal family would have been one of the richest in Europe. But he did not. He gave some land away to his favourites. For instance, Lord Russell, a courtier from Dorset, was given the lands of Tavistock Abbey in Devon and Woburn Abbey in Bedfordshire. These estates were very large, and Russell's descendants, the Dukes of Bedford, have been among the richest landowners in Britain.

But Henry needed so much money that he sold most of the monastic land to the highest bidder. Rich landowners and merchants bought most of it.

As a rule the commissioners sold the land on condition that the buildings were destroyed, and the Russells pulled down Woburn Abbey and built themselves a fine new house on the site. Usually, however, the newcomers stripped the lead from the roofs and sold it, leaving the buildings to fall slowly into ruins. Often local builders pulled down the walls to use the stone as building material.

In a few cases the buildings were saved. William Stumpe, who bought the abbeys at Malmesbury and Osney, converted them both into cloth factories. The citizens of Tewkesbury bought the old abbey building to use as their parish church, and at Durham the monastery was used for the cathedral clergy to live in.

So in a few places the old abbey buildings still stand today. But in most cases only the foundations and a few fragments are left. More than 500 of the finest buildings in the country were either deliberately destroyed or allowed to fall into ruins.

▼ Henry VIII ordered that a Bible in English should be placed in every church for the people to read. In many churches they were chained in place to stop them being stolen

The contents of the monasteries were also sold. Rich merchants and landowners bought books, pictures, and gold or silver plate. Most of these riches have disappeared without trace.

A Wiltshire gentleman, John Aubrey, remembered that in 1630 William Stumpe's great-grandson, then rector of Malmesbury, still had some manuscripts from the abbey. But whenever the rector brewed a barrel of beer he used to plug the bung hole with a sheet of the old parchment, and his sons used the manuscripts to clean their guns. By 1646 they had all gone.

The life of the monks after the dissolution

When the monasteries were dissolved the monks and nuns lost their homes. They were paid pensions as compensation. The abbot of the

rich abbey at Bury St Edmunds got £330 a year, and other abbots were paid between £20 and £200, depending on the size of their abbeys. But ordinary monks only got between £4 and £5 a year—about what a labourer earned. Some monks drew their pensions for many years. The last one died in 1607, more than 60 years later.

A few monks and nuns tried to carry on their old way of life. Four or five monks from the abbey at Monk Bretton in Yorkshire took books from the abbey library, pooled their pensions, and lived together in a house nearby, still observing the rules of their order. Six nuns from Kirklees Abbey in Yorkshire did the same. But most monks looked for some way to earn money, as their pensions were not enough to live on.

Many monks found jobs as parish priests and curates, and at least thirty abbots later became bishops. Some monks abandoned the Church altogether, married and became farmers or merchants.

Other results of the dissolution

The disappearance of the monasteries affected many ordinary people. Travellers had fewer places to stay, there were fewer schools and the poor and needy had fewer places to go for help. But as time passed new inns were built, and new

▲ This gold-plated silver chalice was found when Pillaton Hall in Staffordshire was demolished. It probably belonged to the priory of St Thomas in Stafford, and was taken to Pillaton after the priory was closed down

schools and hospitals were founded to take the place of the monasteries.

In the long run Henry himself gained very little from the dissolution of the monasteries. In the last few years of his reign he spent well over £2 million on wars. They swallowed up all the money he got from selling monastic lands, and much more besides. In 1545 his treasury was empty. 'I am at my wits' end how we shall possibly shift for the three months following,' wrote Thomas Wriothesley, the Lord Chancellor, and Henry had to borrow money at high rates of interest in order to pay his soldiers.

The people who gained most from the dissolution were the merchants and landowners who bought monastic land at reasonable prices. They were proud of their new lands, and they were determined not to give them up. So they opposed any suggestion that the power of the Pope should be restored in England. They feared that if it was, he might want the church lands back.

Study

Use your imagination

1 Brother Michael is a monk at Tintern Abbey. Write an account of how his life changed when Cromwell's men closed the monastery in 1535.
   Things to write about:
   Cromwell's commissioners tell the monks to leave Tintern.
   Brother Michael becomes Michael Richardson, sets up an inn and gets married.
   Ten years after he left Tintern, he returns with his wife and son to look at the ruins.
   (Think of somewhere you left when your life changed, that you later revisited.)

2 Robert Blackstock is a wealthy merchant. Write an account of how he became even richer when he bought a small monastery and its land.
   Things to write about:
   Blackstock buys the monastery land and buildings.
   The buildings are pulled down.
   The land is used for sheep grazing.
   Blackstock builds a fine new house for himself and his family.
   (Think of a time when you had the chance to buy something you wanted more cheaply than usual.)

3 Write an account showing how the life of a man or woman was changed when a monastery was closed. For example, you might choose a man who joined the Pilgrimage of Grace or someone who had hoped to go on a pilgrimage to Becket's shrine.
   Things to write about:
   His or her occupation before and after the monastery was closed.
   His or her views on whether or not closing the monasteries was a change for the better.
   (Think of how the closing of a place of work, or a place where you enjoyed going, affected your life.)

The King's power after the dissolution

The fall of Thomas Cromwell

Thomas Cromwell served Henry VIII well. He helped him to get his divorce, organised the dissolution of the monasteries, and helped to modernise the system of government. In 1540 Henry made him Earl of Essex, and he seemed to be the most powerful man in the country.

But Cromwell had many enemies at court. They knew that if he lost the King's favour he would be dismissed. Their chance came in 1540 when Thomas arranged for Henry to marry Anne of Cleves. Henry disliked her from the moment he saw her, and blamed Cromwell.

Led by the Duke of Norfolk, Cromwell's enemies set to work. They persuaded Henry that Thomas was plotting against him and was also trying to alter the beliefs of the Church. Henry was very upset by these accusations. Though he had destroyed the power of the Pope in England, he did not want to alter the Church's teaching. So one day in June 1540, as Cromwell sat with the Council, he was arrested, and imprisoned. A few days later he was executed for treason. Lord Darcy's prophecy, made at his own trial in 1537, had come true.

The end of Henry's reign

Henry himself died in 1547. By seizing control of the Church and breaking the power of the great landowners, he had made the English monarchy more powerful than ever before. At about the same time the rulers of France, Spain and parts of Germany were doing much the same as Henry. In all these countries the power of the King grew, while that of the Church and the landowners declined.

Study

The power of the Crown

1 (a) Read the section on 'The fall of Thomas Cromwell' above.
  (b) Copy the statement below that you think is correct:
  > Henry destroyed the power of the Pope in England so that he could change the beliefs of the Church.
  > Henry destroyed the power of the Pope in England but he did not want to change the beliefs of the Church.

2 Look at the picture of the chained Bible on page 76 and read the caption above it. At the beginning of Henry's reign it was against the law of the Church to read the Bible in English. How did Henry use his power as the head of the Church to encourage ordinary people to read the Bible?

3 Read the sections on 'The fall of Thomas Cromwell' and 'The end of Henry's reign'.

Copy the statements below and complete each of them by adding an example:
> The King had the power to arrest and execute ministers, for example ...
> Henry was more powerful at the end of his reign than at the beginning, for example ...
> The Kings in other countries were also becoming more powerful, for example ...

Further work

Charts, maps and diagrams

Date	Event
1533	Act of _____ Henry becomes head of the English Church
____	Act closing smaller monasteries
1536	Pilgrimage of _____ tries to stop Henry closing _____ monasteries
1539	Act closing large monasteries
____	All monasteries closed by this date

▲ Henry gains control over the Church

1 Time chart
(a) Copy the time chart above.
(b) Fill in the gaps. You will find the information you need between pages 56 and 76.
(c) Copy the statement that you think is the more accurate:

> Parliament co-operated with the King when he closed down the monasteries.
> Parliament opposed the King when he tried to close down the monasteries.

2 Annotated map: the shires and the realm
When Henry described Lincolnshire as 'one of the most brute and beastly shires of the whole realm', he was saying that it was a poor county and the people there were not much better than animals.
(a) Look at the annotated map on page 75. Then draw the outline of England and Wales using the map at the beginning of this book.
(b) Annotate your map to show the region of England which had
    the wealthier counties,
    the poorer counties.
(c) Wales was divided into counties and brought under English law in 1536. Add this information to your map.

3 Scatter diagram: the results of the dissolution of the monasteries
(a) Copy the diagram below.
(b) Write short notes below each box showing the effect that the closing of the monasteries had on different people.

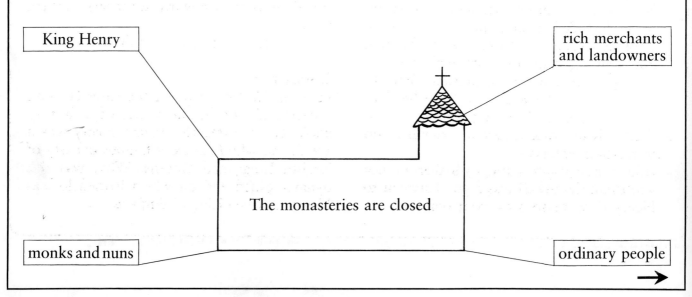

Writing

Extracts from letters and reports

1 Copy the three extracts below. They are taken from letters or reports written during the reign of Henry VIII.

(a) 'As for the abbot ... he delighted much in playing dice and cards ... '(Page 67.)

(b) '... most humbly I beseech you to take in good part whatsoever promises I shall make unto the rebels ... for surely I shall observe [keep] no part thereof.' (Page 72.)

(c) 'I am at my wits' end how we shall possibly shift [manage] for the three months following.' (Page 78.)

2 Answer the following questions about each extract, writing complete sentences:

(d) Who wrote it?

(e) Whom was it written to?

(f) Whom or what was it written about?

Henry's character

Henry VIII once said, 'If I thought my cap knew my thoughts I would throw it in the fire.'

1 Copy the sentence above. Then write one or two sentences saying what, in your opinion, the statement shows about Henry's character.

2 Find and copy two more statements that were spoken or written by Henry VIII. What, in your opinion, does each of them show about his character?

Biography of Thomas Cromwell

1 Make a list of four important events that you would include in a biography or life story of Thomas Cromwell. Write key words only. For example, your first note might be:

1532   Advised H. to persuade Parl. to make King not Pope head of Church of Eng.

2 Write his biography, turning your list into interesting sentences.

3 Add a paragraph stating whether or not you think Cromwell was a good servant to Henry. Give reasons for your opinion.

Oral work: treason trials

During the reign of Henry VIII the following people were imprisoned and tried for committing treason against the King:

Thomas More   Ann Boleyn   Robert Aske

1 Choose one of the people above. Write a speech (of about a minute), that he or she might have made when charged with treason.

Things to write about:

What the 'prisoner' had done or not done to be charged with treason.

His or her reason for claiming that the charge is false.

2 Choose three people, one representing each prisoner, to make his or her speech to the class. At the end of each speech the 'prisoner' may be questioned by up to three members of the class.

3 When all three prisoners have been tried, take a vote on each case to decide whether or not the prisoner is guilty of treason.

Quiz

True or false?

Henry VIII had eight wives. F

Henry ordered that a Bible in English should be placed in every church. T

After he sold the monasteries and their lands, Henry was never short of money again. F

Make up two 'True or false?' questions and write them on separate sheets of paper. Hand them in and hold the quiz. F/T

Glossary

Write the following words in your glossary, and explain in your own words what each of them means:

realm   policy   dissolution

Library work

Look up *Henry VII* under the letter H in an encyclopedia or in the index of a history book on the sixteenth century. Henry was a Welshman who founded a famous dynasty of English Kings and Queens. What was this dynasty called and on which battlefield was Henry crowned King of England?

Tudor / ?

4 Inquiry: The strangers come to Britain

Introduction

While Henry VIII was increasing his power over the English Church, Christians in other parts of Europe were also quarrelling with the Pope. These quarrels, and the great changes that took place because of them, are known as the *Reformation* and the *Counter-Reformation*. One way to find out about these important events is to study the story of one man who took part in them.

The stranger in the Book of Martyrs

Brighton is a large holiday town on the coast of Sussex. Most visitors never see the old parish church of St Nicholas because it is hidden by a mass of modern buildings. In the days when Brighton was a small fishing village, men at sea, returning with their catch, could see the church clearly. It stood on a low ridge of downland behind the cottages of the town, and when the fishermen sighted it they knew that they would soon be home.

In 1571, when Elizabeth was Queen of England, a copy of a large book, called the *Book of Martyrs*, was placed in every cathedral and in some parish churches. The book contained a collection of stories about English men and women who were put to death between 1555 and 1558 because they did not agree with the teaching of the Catholic Church, and would not pretend that they did.

The fishermen and their families already knew one of the stories. Deryk Carver, who was burnt at the stake at Lewes in 1555, had lived in Brighton, or *Brighthelmstone* as it was then called. Many people would have remembered him. Some of them had probably walked across the downs to Lewes to see him executed. In 1570 one of Carver's sons still lived in Brighton. Unlike most of the fishermen, he was an educated man who could read the stories in the *Book of Martyrs* for himself.

For the next hundred years, the *Book of Martyrs* was widely read in England. It was the book that many people treasured most after the Bible. But Deryk Carver was not an Englishman. He was a foreigner, or as the people of the time would have said, a stranger. Later in the sixteenth century, and again in the seventeenth century, thousands of strangers who shared Carver's beliefs settled in Britain.

John Foxe, who wrote the *Book of Martyrs*, wanted his readers to remember the courage of the men and women whose stories he had collected. He goes into great detail when he describes how Carver died, but he does not tell us much about the martyr's life before he was arrested and executed. This inquiry will try to find out more about Carver and the strangers who came after him, by following the clues that Foxe gives us in his book.

---

1 In which year was a copy of Foxe's *Book of Martyrs* placed in every cathedral?
2 In which year was Deryk Carver executed?
3 Why may some of the people of Brighthelmstone have known more about Carver's life than John Foxe did?

What do you think?

Why may John Foxe have gone into great detail about Carver's death instead of saying more about his life as a whole?

The stranger's native country
Extract 1

> '... born in the village of Dilson, by Stockham, in the land of Liège ...'
> (From the story of Deryk Carver in Foxe's *Book of Martyrs*)

1 Compare the extract from Foxe with the map opposite. Which country did Deryk Carver come from?

▼ Northern Europe, showing Flanders in the sixteenth century

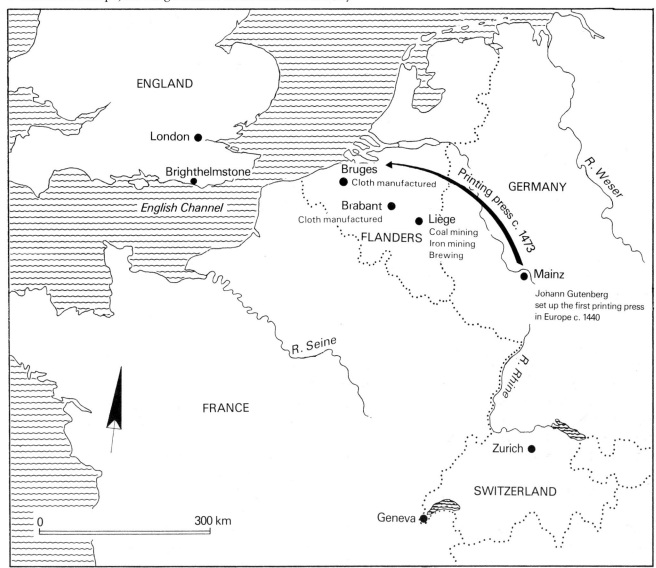

2 Give three examples of the kind of work Carver would have seen going on in his area.

3 (a) Name three countries whose merchants might have gone to Bruges and Brabant to buy cloth.

(b) In which of these countries did Johann Gutenberg set up the first printing press in Europe?

(c) By which year had the printing press reached Flanders?

What do you think?

Which of these statements do you think is the more accurate?

(a) Deryk Carver came from an industrial country. He was probably a skilled workman who could read and write.

(b) Deryk Carver came from an industrial country. He was probably a skilled workman and it is unlikely that he could read and write.

Give reasons for your answer.

The stranger and the Protestants

While Deryk Carver was growing up near Liège, great changes were taking place in the countries around Flanders. Instead of being united in one Catholic Church, Christians were beginning to split up and form new churches. The people who joined these churches were called Protestants, or protesters, because they objected to obeying a Pope whom they did not respect and did not want to follow the teaching of a church they no longer agreed with.

Table 1

Date	Protestant leader	Place
1521	Martin Luther	Saxony in Germany
1522	Ulrich Zwingli	Zurich in Switzerland
1536	John Calvin (a Frenchman)	Geneva in Switzerland
1542	Calvin's teaching spread to Flanders	

Table 1 shows you who the three most important Protestant leaders were, and the places where they set up their churches.

We are told by Foxe that Carver was about forty years old in 1555.

1 In what year was Carver born?
2 How old was he when Calvin set up his church in Geneva?
3 How old was he when Calvin's teaching spread to Flanders?

Table 2

	Catholic Church	Protestant Churches	
		Lutherans	Calvinists and Zwinglians
Head of the Church	The Pope	The ruler of each country	People elected by each church congregation
The Bible	In Latin. The priest should explain its teaching to the people.	In the language of the ordinary people of each country	In the language of the ordinary people of each country
Services	In Latin	In the language that people usually spoke	In the language that people usually spoke
Priests	Priests are set apart from ordinary people. They are needed to hold the service of the Mass and the other sacraments that help people find God.	Priests hold the services and give advice, but ordinary people can find God by praying to him and listening to their consciences.	No priests. Ministers lead the congregations in the services and in studying the Bible, but must listen to the views of the congregation.

Table 2 shows you the differences between the Churches.

Reading *across* the table, find the heading 'Catholic Church'.

Reading *down* the left-hand side of the table, find 'The Bible'.

1 What language did Catholics believe the Bible should be written in and who did they think should explain it to ordinary people?
2 What language did the Protestants think the Bible should be written in?
3 Why were priests less important in the Protestant Church than in the Catholic Church?

The German Emperor and the Protestants

The German Emperor, Charles V, ruled over the princes of Germany and the merchants and workmen of Flanders. He was afraid that if his subjects broke away from the Catholic Church they would also start breaking away from his Empire, and this would cause wars.

Charles was not powerful enough to stop Lutheranism from spreading in Germany but he was determined to stamp out Calvinism in Flanders. He encouraged the Catholic bishops to use their authority to arrest people who they suspected were Protestants. If the suspects would not promise to obey the Pope and follow the teaching of the Catholic Church, they were burnt to death, in front of crowds of people.

1 What did Charles think would happen to his Empire if his subjects set up their own churches?
2 Which churchmen had the authority to arrest people who were suspected of being Protestants?
3 What happened to Protestants who were arrested if they would not give up their beliefs?

What do you think?
Foxe tells us that Deryk Carver and his family came to Brighthelmstone in about 1546. Think of what happened to Carver in 1555 and what was happening in Flanders in the 1540s. Why may Carver have decided to leave Flanders?

The stranger and his family settle in Brighthelmstone

Extract 2

'... Deryk Carver, beer-brewer of Brighthelmstead [Brighthelmstone] in the county of Sussex.'
(From the story of Deryk Carver in Foxe's *Book of Martyrs*)

Tea and coffee were unknown in England before the seventeenth century. Instead, people drank large quantities of ale, which they brewed from the malt that they extracted from barley.

In the fifteenth century, the people in the south of England began to import a new drink from Holland and Flanders. This drink was called beer, and it was darker and more bitter than ale because hops, which were not grown in England, had been added to the brew. Beer was not brewed in England until about 1524, when immigrants from Flanders started planting fields of hops in Kent.

At first, some people who did not like the new drink said that it was un-English and unhealthy, but gradually beer became as popular as ale with people in the south.

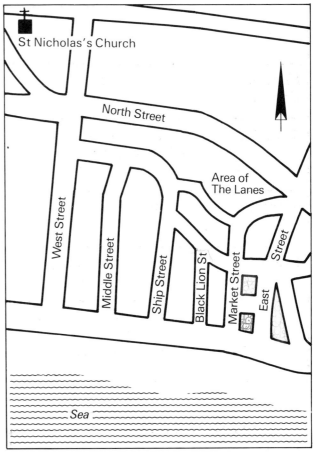

▼ Sixteenth-century Brighton

1 (a) What does Foxe say that Deryk Carver did for a living?
(b) The Black Lion was the emblem of Flanders. In Brighton today, there is a plaque to show where Carver set up in business. In which street would you look for it?

85

2 (a) Look at the map of south-east England. What was added to the malt to make beer?

(b) Why was it easier for beer brewers in England to obtain supplies after 1524?

3 (a) Where did the fishing fleet from Brighthelmstone go to catch herrings?

(b) The herrings were dried or salted to preserve them. Why would people who ate them want plenty to drink with their meals?

What do you think?

Why may Deryk Carver have thought that Brighthelmstone would be a good place for him to set up in business?

The stranger is arrested

When Deryk Carver and his family first came to England, King Henry VIII was still alive. When Henry died in 1547, his young son, Edward, became King. Edward's advisers were Protestants, and one of them, Archbishop Cranmer, wrote a Prayer Book in English which had to be used in every church.

Edward died in 1553, when he was only sixteen years old, and his stepsister, Mary, became Queen.

Table 3 shows you some important events from the first three years of Mary's reign.

Extract 3

> 'He said that since the Queen's coronation he had ... that Bible ... read in his house.'
> (From the story of Deryk Carver in Foxe's *Book of Martyrs*)

Table 3

1553	Mary turned out the Protestant bishops and put Catholics in their place. Church services were held in Latin.
1554	Some Protestants rebelled when Mary announced that she was going to marry Philip of Spain, a Catholic. The rebels were defeated. Mary married Philip.
1555	The persecution of Protestants began.

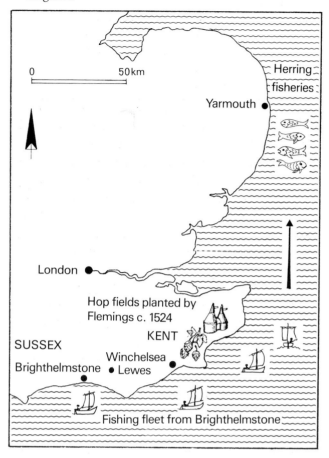

▼ Brighthelmstone and the industries of south-east England

1 Why were Deryk Carver and his family safe in England until 1553?

2 Queen Mary did not persecute the Protestants at the beginning of her reign. What happened in 1554 to make her treat them more harshly?

3 Carver and twelve other men were arrested when they were holding a meeting at his house at the end of October 1554.

(a) Look at Extract 3 and Table 3. What had Carver been doing that was against the law?

(b) Mary was crowned Queen in 1553. For about how many months had Carver been breaking the law when he was arrested?

What do you think?

Carver and his family could have left England when Mary became Queen. What reasons may he have had for deciding to stay in Brighthelmstone?

The stranger is burnt at the stake
Extract 4

> '... when he came to the signe of the
> Starre the people drew near unto him.'
> (From the story of Deryk Carver in
> Foxe's *Book of Martyrs*)

Deryk Carver was taken to London and kept in Newgate Prison for seven months before he was tried and condemned to death. His execution was fixed for 22 July 1555 and he was taken to Lewes, the county town of Sussex, to be burnt at the stake.

On the morning of his execution Carver came up from the cellars of the building where he had been imprisoned, carrying an English Bible. While he knelt to pray, one of the guards threw the Bible into the barrel in which Carver was to be burnt to death. Carver climbed into the barrel. Before his guards could tie him to the stake, he picked up the Bible and tried to save it by throwing it to the crowd.

The sheriff knew that many of the people were on Carver's side and that someone in the crowd might hide the Bible. He shouted that anyone caught trying to hide the Bible would be executed too, and ordered the people to throw the book back, to be burnt with Carver.

Extract 5

> 'In the vaults below this building were
> imprisoned ten of the seventeen
> Protestant martyrs burned at the stake
> within a few yards of this site.'
> (From the plaque on the Town Hall, Lewes.
> The Town Hall is built on the site of
> the Star Inn)

1 (a) Look at Extract 4 and Extract 5. What was the name of the inn where Carver was imprisoned?

(b) What modern building now stands over the cellars?

2 (a) How far was the inn from the place where Carver was executed?

(b) Look at the map and find the inn. Why may this part of Lewes have been chosen for the site of the execution?

3 (a) Why was it so important to Carver to save the Bible?

(b) Why was it so important to the sheriff to destroy the Bible?

▼ Lewes High Street, from a map made in 1620

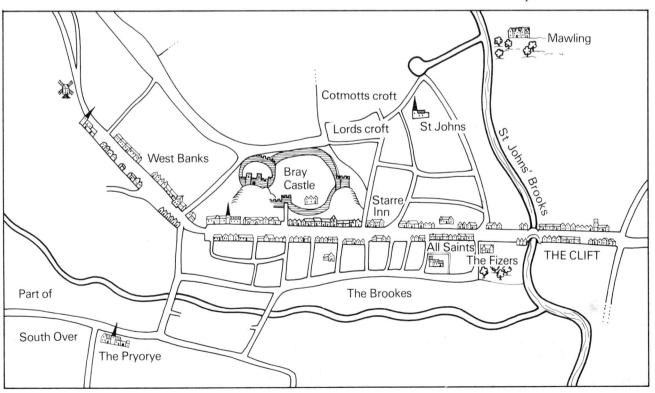

What do you think?

Queen Mary, who was a Catholic, persecuted the Protestants by having them burnt at the stake for heresy. Queen Elizabeth, who was a Protestant, persecuted the Catholics by having them hanged, drawn and quartered for treason.

1 (a) Which Queen ruled England when Foxe published the *Book of Martyrs*?

   (b) Was she a Catholic or a Protestant?

2 Propaganda is information spread by a government or other organisation to try to persuade people to support its cause. Was Foxe's book a piece of Protestant propaganda? Give reasons for your answer.

3 Which of these statements do you think is the more accurate?

   Propaganda does not give the facts about what really happened.

   Propaganda may tell us the facts but only from one point of view.

   Give examples from Foxe's *Book of Martyrs* to illustrate your answer.

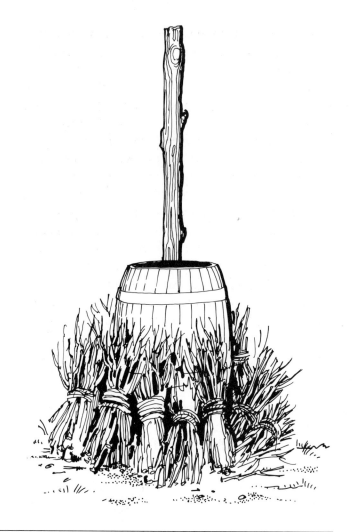

▶ A stake, barrel and brushwood—used when heretics were burnt

---

The strangers become British

Extract 6

> 'To the country of the Briton, the Saxons brought their industry, the Northmen their energy and the Flemings and French their skill and spirit of liberty; and out of the whole has come the English nation.'
> (From *The Huguenots in England and Ireland* by Samuel Smiles. Published 1889)

Twenty years after Deryk Carver was arrested in Brighthelmstone, Protestant refugee families from Flanders and France were again landing on the coast of Sussex. They had come to escape from the fighting that was going on in their own countries between Catholics and Protestants. They had to leave most of their possessions behind and arrived in England with the few belongings that they could carry. England was a Protestant country again, ruled by Mary's half-sister, Elizabeth, so the refugees thought they would not be turned away.

The people of the Sussex towns felt sorry for the foreign Protestants and helped them, but hoped that they would soon move away and find work.

Because many of the refugees were skilled craftsmen, they were able to earn their own living and support their families, once they had found a place where they could settle. Many cloth workers from Flanders went to Yorkshire, and silk manufacturers from France set up workshops in London. Among the French and Flemings there were gardeners who knew how to grow the new flowers and vegetables that were coming into Europe from overseas. Some of them settled in Essex and the eastern counties of England and helped to develop the gardens there.

The French refugees were called *Huguenots*. This name spread to the Flemings, though usually the English called them *strangers*.

When they first arrived in Britain, the strangers kept together and formed their own churches. But as they spread out through the country, looking for work, they began to join English churches and marry English people.

Some people today, who can trace their families back to their Huguenot ancestors, belong to the Huguenot Society, which is based in London. People with the following surnames may be descended from Huguenots:

    Morel   Guppy   Maynard   *Erny*
    Spiller   Gerard   Stocker   *Sousson*

The spelling of other names has changed. For example, 'Wallacher' was the Flemish name given to a skilled workman who 'fulled' or cleaned and finished the woven cloth. As time went by, the name Wallacher changed to Walker.

By the time Samuel Smiles wrote his book in 1889, the Huguenots were no longer strangers, but part of the British people.

Look at Extract 6.

1 Name two parts of Great Britain where the Huguenots settled.

2 (a) What does Samuel Smiles say the Flemish and French Huguenots brought to Britain?

(b) Give two or three examples that he might have used to prove his point.

3 The Huguenots began emigrating to Britain in large numbers from about 1575.

(a) For roughly how many centuries had the Huguenots formed part of Britain's population by the time that Samuel Smiles wrote his book about them?

(b) Name two or three groups of people from abroad who have settled in Britain since the book was published.

What do you think?

1 Why would life have been difficult for the Huguenots when they first arrived in Britain?

2 Once they had settled into their new homes, did they make Britain more or less prosperous? Give reasons for your answer.

OUT OF 89 MARKS

▲ A Tudor merchant and his wife

5 The English go abroad

A voyage to Newfoundland

In April 1536 two ships, the *Trinity* and the *Minion*, set sail from Gravesend in Kent. There were about 120 men on board. Ninety were sailors. The rest were the sons of lawyers and landowners. These young men were paying for the hire of the boats, and the crews' wages.

The leader of the expedition was a brave and well-educated man named Horne. He and his friends wanted to explore the island of Newfoundland, discovered in 1497 by John Cabot. Since then, fishing boats had visited it regularly to catch cod which swarmed off the coast. But nobody had bothered to explore inland.

Adventures on the way

For two months the little ships sailed westward down the Channel and across the Atlantic. Then, at the beginning of July, the sailors sighted land. It was Cape Breton, and as they steered north-east to reach Newfoundland they came upon a small rocky island covered with sea birds. They landed, killed as many birds as they could and took their eggs. Then one of the crew saw several black bears. He guided men armed with bows and arrows to the spot, and they shot several of the animals.

For the rest of the day they were all busy skinning and cooking the birds and bears they had killed. It was the first fresh meat they had eaten since they had left England. After the salt pork they had been eating it tasted delicious.

They explore the island

A few days later the ships reached Newfoundland and anchored off shore. Each morning the men landed and explored. Every night they returned to the ships to sleep.

One morning a London merchant named Daubeny came on deck and saw a canoe full of Indians paddling towards the two ships. He called his friends to come and look. The crew of the *Minion* launched a boat to go to meet the Indians, but they turned and paddled away, and were soon out of sight round a headland.

A number of the explorers landed and searched for the Indians. They found their campsite with the fire still alight and half a bear roasting over it. But the Indians had gone, leaving behind them only a boot trimmed with fur and a large warm leather glove. The explorers took these back to their ships. They never saw any sign of the Indians again.

The sailors turn cannibal

As the weeks passed the explorers began to run short of food. They tried to hunt and fish but they caught little or nothing. So they had to live on roots, herbs and shellfish. It was not enough, and they grew hungry and thin.

One day two sailors were out searching for

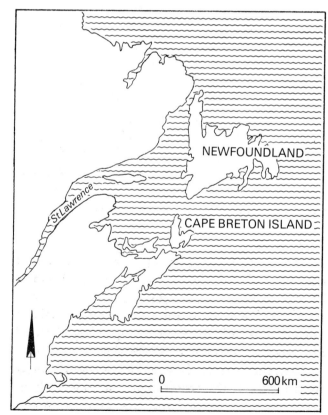

▲ The coast of north America in 1536

90

food. As one was struggling to dig up a root the other struck him down and killed him. Then he cut flesh from the body, cooked it and ate it.

He told one or two of his friends what he had done. They decided to join forces, and every few days they killed and ate one of the other sailors. The officers knew that some of the crew were disappearing, but they assumed that wild beasts or Indians had killed them.

The officers find out

One day an officer went to search for food. To his surprise he smelt meat cooking. He followed the scent and found a sailor sitting beside a fire eating roast meat. The officer took it for granted that the man had trapped an animal, and was angry because he had not shared it out. At first the sailor said nothing, but in the end, as the officer continued to accuse him of being selfish, he shouted, 'If thou wouldst need know, the meat I had was a piece of a man.'

Horne appeals to the sailors

The officer went back to the ships and told Horne what had happened. Horne called all the members of the expedition together. He told them they were all in God's hands, and that it was better to trust Him to help than to try to relieve their hunger by killing one another, risking eternal damnation and burning for ever, body and soul, in the everlasting fires of Hell.

The men listened, but they were not convinced. They knew they could not possibly find enough food to stock up their ships for the journey home, so unless help arrived they would stay where they were and starve. So they decided to draw lots. The losers would be killed and eaten. This would perhaps enable the others to live long enough to be rescued.

The rescue

As the meeting broke up one of the crew looked out to sea. To his delight he saw a ship. It was a French boat, and that night it anchored close at hand. At dead of night some English sailors rowed alongside the French ship. They climbed aboard and overpowered the sleeping crew.

Then they went below and found good stocks of provisions. They took them and loaded them on board the *Trinity* and the *Minion*. When they had finished they set sail for England.

▼ An American Indian in ceremonial dress, drawn by John White, governor of Virginia, in 1587

The return home

They sailed back by a northerly route past high icebergs and flocks of great white birds. In October they landed in Cornwall and went home. When one of them, Thomas Butts, got home to Norfolk he was so thin that his father, Sir William, did not recognise him. Thomas had to show him a birthmark on his leg to prove he was his son.

Afterwards many members of the expedition held important posts at the King's court or in the city of London. But none of them ever forgot their voyage to Newfoundland.

How do we know?

Hakluyt's *Voyages*

You can read the story of Horne's voyage to Newfoundland in *The Principal Navigations, Voyages, Traffics and Discoveries of the English People* by Richard Hakluyt, which was published in 1589.

When Hakluyt was born in England in 1552, Portugal and Spain were two of the richest countries in Europe. Much of their wealth came from the trade they carried on with their empires overseas. They were able to build up these empires because their sailors had explored the oceans of the world and opened up new trade routes. Hakluyt went to work in France when he was a young man and was annoyed to find that the people there did not have a very high opinion of the English. They said that English sailors were not as good as the Portuguese and Spanish because they had never made an important voyage. Hakluyt was determined to prove that English sailors were as good as any in the world, so he collected all the stories he could find about English seamen and explorers, going back for hundreds of years, and put them in his book. In 1588, when his work was nearly finished, the English defeated a fleet that the King of Spain sent to invade England. Hakluyt mentioned this great victory at the end of his book because he thought it proved his point.

Hakluyt's *Voyages*, as the book became known, became popular in England. It made the English feel proud of what their countrymen had achieved in the past and helped them to believe that they could do just as well in the future.

1 (a) In which book can you read the story of Horne's voyage to Newfoundland?
  (b) In what year was the book published?
2 Consider what we are told in the story.
  (a) In what year did Horne go on his voyage?
  (b) How may Hakluyt have found out what happened on the voyage?

3 (a) What made Hakluyt decide to write his book?
  (b) Why may the English victory at sea in 1588 have made people want to read Hakluyt's book when it was published in 1589?

What do you think?

Propaganda is information we spread in order to convince people that our aims and ideas are right. Is Hakluyt's *Voyages* propaganda? Give reasons for your answer.

Dr Dee's map

In the British Library in London there is a large map drawn on fine parchment. It shows the eastern coastline of north America, from Newfoundland in the north to the Gulf of Mexico in the south. A Welshman called Dr John Dee drew the map in about 1580, when Hakluyt and several other Englishmen were planning to send a group of people to set up the first English colony in America. They asked Dr Dee to help them by drawing a map that would show the settlers what the American coastline was like, and where the best place to start a colony might be.

Dr Dee was the best map-maker in England. When he was young, no one in England understood map-making, so he went to Flanders where he was taught by Gerard Mercator, the greatest cartographer or map-maker living at that time. When Dr Dee returned to England he brought with him a collection of the kind of scientific equipment that was used by the Flemish cartographers. He set up this equipment at his home at Mortlake, near London. Many important Englishmen who wanted to build up England's power at sea came to watch Dr Dee at work, and to ask his advice.

1 Where is Dr Dee's map kept today?
2 Why did Dr Dee go to Flanders to learn map-making?

3 In the middle of the sixteenth century, people in Europe said that, compared with the Portuguese and Spanish, English sailors had not achieved very much. Consider the time chart opposite. What reason or reasons may they have had for forming this opinion of the English?

What do you think?
The work of Richard Hakluyt and Dr Dee helped the English to feel confident that they would be able to build up an empire overseas. Explain why.

1536	Horne's sailors explore parts of Newfoundland but do not settle there.
1547	Dr Dee has to go to Flanders to learn map-making.
1580	Hakluyt and other Englishmen plan the first English colony in America.
1588	English sailors defeat the Spanish fleet sent to invade England.
1589	Hakluyt's *Voyages* is published.

Understanding what happened

1 (a) Horne's voyage to Newfoundland and back took about six months. Copy the time chart below and fill in the month when each event happened. You will find some of the months are given in the story. You will have to work out the others.

Date	Event
——	The *Trinity* and *Minion* sail from Gravesend.
——	Horne reaches Cape Breton and sails N.E. to Newfoundland.
——	Indians are seen but disappear.
——	The crew turns to cannibalism.
——	The French ship arrives. The English plunder it.
——	The *Trinity* and *Minion* reach Cornwall.

(b) Why did Horne go to Newfoundland?
(c) Why did Thomas Butts have to prove who he was when he reached home?

2 (a) Which men on the expedition did not know how to sail a ship but paid the crews' wages? Did they form an eighth, a quarter or three-quarters of the total number of men on the expedition?
(b) Why did some of the crew disappear when the *Trinity* and *Minion* reached Newfoundland?
(c) What plan did the crew put forward after Horne had asked them to trust in God?

3 (a) Give two examples to show that it was possible to find food. Why were the Englishmen unable to live on it?
(b) Give an example to show that the Indians of Newfoundland knew how to survive in the harsh climate.
(c) Give two examples to show that the Indians of Newfoundland deliberately avoided the Englishmen.

What do you think?
Why was a voyage of exploration more likely to be successful if the explorers made friends with the people whose country they were exploring?

TOTAL : 62

Further work

Writing

1 Captain Horne would have kept a log book in which each day he wrote an account of what happened on his voyage. Write four or more entries that might have appeared in the log book of the *Trinity*.
2 Tell the story of the voyage as Thomas Butt might have told it to his parents when he was well again.
3 Some Indian tribes have had stories handed down to them, describing how the white men came to America. Tell the story of Horne's men as it might be told today by an Indian.

Drawing

1 Draw the map of the north American coastline on page 90. Write one or two sentences explaining why English sailors needed maps when they began to sail across the Atlantic.
2 Draw the picture of an American Indian in Virginia on page 91. Write one or two sentences explaining how Dr Dee's map helped Englishmen who were planning to settle in America.
3 Draw an illustration of an incident from Horne's voyage that might be used for a modern edition of Hakluyt's *Voyages*. Write one or two sentences explaining why Hakluyt wrote his book.

Mime

Divide the class into five or six groups. Divide the story of Horne's voyage into five or six sections. Give each group a section of the story to present as a scene in a mime. Each scene should last about two minutes. When you have prepared the scenes, perform them, in the order in which they happen in the story, in front of the class.

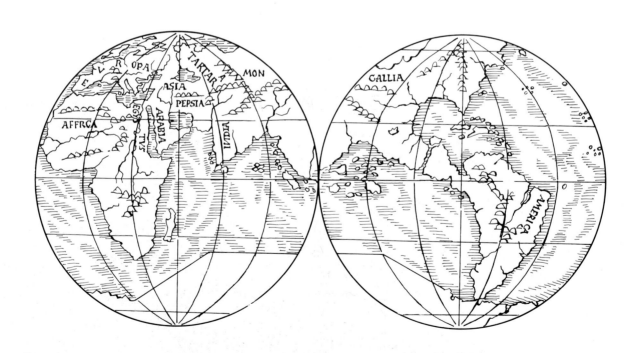

▲ These hemispheres or half-globes are based on a pair drawn in about 1527 by a monk living in Flanders

Seaways to the east

The new ships

At the beginning of the fifteenth century ships were badly designed. They were oval in shape, about twice as long as they were wide. At each end they were built up high out of the water. This made them top-heavy. They were difficult to steer, and a sudden gust of wind from the side could blow them over. It was impossible to make long voyages in such ships.

The Spanish and Portuguese were the best shipbuilders, and gradually began to design better ships. They were long and narrow, and the 'castles' at the front and back were made much lower. They were easy to steer and could sail through violent storms without capsizing. So they were suitable for long voyages.

Portuguese and Spanish sailors began to explore the seas in their new ships. They wanted above all to find an easy route to the East Indies to buy the spices which people wanted to flavour their food.

The dangers of ocean navigation

Ocean voyages were still difficult and dangerous. By carefully observing the sun and stars a captain could work out the latitude of his ship's position, but he had no way to find out its longitude. So when a ship was out of sight of land the captain could only guess where he was. When he sighted land and tried to find a harbour there were very few accurate charts to rely on. As a result many ships were wrecked on hidden rocks and reefs close to the shore.

Diseases at sea

Most ships were small and cramped, and diseases spread quickly. Anthony Ingram went on a voyage to Benin in Africa. He wrote that nine of the crew died of fever, and the rest were so weak that they could hardly raise the anchor or set the sails.

Some diseases were caused by food poisoning. The diet on board ship was plain and

▲ The *Jesus of Lubeck* had high forecastles and sterncastles. Henry VIII bought her second-hand in 1544. She leaked so badly that fish used to swim about in her hold. She sank in a battle in 1568

monotonous, consisting of salt pork, beef or fish with cheese and ship's biscuits washed down with water, beer or wine. The only fresh food was fish, seals, shellfish, sea birds and penguins caught by the crew.

Sometimes if the wind dropped a ship might be becalmed in the middle of the ocean, stranded far from land. Food and water soon ran short, and the crew starved. But even if there was plenty of salt meat and biscuits the sailors soon fell sick with scurvy because they had no vitamin C, which is only found in fresh fruit or vegetables.

Thomas Stevens, on a voyage to India in 1579, described the effects of scurvy. First the sailors' gums began to swell. Then their legs swelled up and the whole of their bodies ached. Gradually they grew weaker, and eventually they died.

In the sixteenth century nobody knew for certain what caused sailors to fall ill, so nobody could do anything to prevent the diseases. On a long voyage it was common for half the crew to die before the ship returned to port.

The profits of trade

In spite of the high death rate, sailors still volunteered to man the ships because they could get more money on one or two successful voyages than many people earned in a lifetime. In western Europe spices were very expensive, but in the East Indies they were plentiful. So a captain and his crew could make an enormous profit by sailing to the Indies, buying a cargo of spices, and bringing it back to sell to merchants in western Europe.

▲ A sixteenth-century astrolabe. It was used to work out the ship's position by taking bearings on the stars

Sailing to the Indies

The galleon

1 (a) Copy the drawing of the caravel below.

(b) Name two countries whose shipbuilders designed ocean-going ships.

(c) Which islands did they hope to reach?

The dangers of ocean navigation

2 (a) Copy out these sentences, using the following words to fill in the gaps correctly:

> latitude find ship captain
> land stars sea sun

It was difficult for a ship's _____ to know where he was at _____ and to _____ his way across the ocean. By observing the _____ and stars he could work out the _____ of the _____ but not the longitude. When he could not see any _____ he had to guess where he was.

▼ A caravel was a small, light, fast ship used by Spanish and Portuguese explorers between 1400 and 1600

(b) Look at the picture of the astrolabe on page 96. What was this instrument used for?

(c) Why were many ships wrecked even when they had sighted land?

Food and diseases at sea

3 (a) Why did European people want spices from the East Indies?

(b) Give an example of each of the following:

(i) a method used to preserve food that was taken on long voyages,

(ii) a disease caused by the lack of fresh food on long voyages.

(c) Why were sailors willing to risk their lives by going on long voyages?

/20

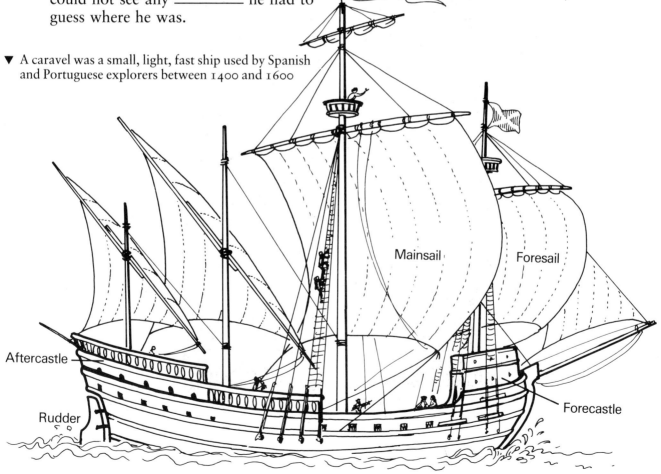

Aftercastle

Rudder

Mainsail

Foresail

Forecastle

Spanish and Portuguese empires

Spanish and Portuguese discoveries

The rulers of Spain and Portugal encouraged their explorers by lending them ships and money. By the end of the fifteenth century the explorers had discovered a sea route to India and landed on the coasts of south and central America. (For details see the table on page 99.) The most important voyage was made by Christopher Columbus in 1492, in ships provided by Queen Isabella of Spain. He wanted to find a new, easy route to the East Indies. He knew that the world was round, so he thought that if he sailed west, he would eventually reach the Indies. He sailed across the Atlantic, and when he sighted land he thought he had reached the Indies. So he called the islands the West Indies, and described the inhabitants as Indians. In fact he had discovered the continent of America.

In 1493 Pope Alexander VI, who was himself a Spaniard, granted Spain complete control over all lands discovered on the other side of the Atlantic Ocean. Soon Spanish soldiers, merchants and priests landed there. In parts of central and south America the Spaniards found prosperous people living in well-planned towns, and with rich gold and silver mines. The Spaniards destroyed the towns, killed the people and shipped the gold and silver back to Spain.

English explorers

At first the English did not bother to try to establish colonies. English merchants had a profitable trade selling woollen cloth to the Netherlands, and could not see any point in spending their money on voyages of exploration which might easily end in disaster.

The only important voyage from England before 1500 was made by John Cabot, an Italian, who set out from Bristol in 1497 with a charter from Henry VII. Cabot believed that if he sailed across the north Atlantic he would eventually reach China. In fact he discovered Newfoundland, which he claimed in the name of King Henry. When he returned to England King Henry gave him a present of £10. But Newfoundland was not nearly so rich as the lands which the Spaniards had discovered further south.

England and Spain, 1509–1577

When the English merchants heard of the wealth which the Spanish had discovered in south America, they decided that it would be worth their while to explore for new lands and establish colonies. Henry VIII encouraged them. He said that the Pope had no right to divide the world up and give so much of it to Spain, and he was pleased when sailors like Horne went to explore America.

But when Henry's daughter, Mary, became Queen in 1553, she changed Henry's policy. She married King Philip of Spain, and ordered English sailors not to go to America. So instead they concentrated on trying to find a route to the east round the north of Russia.

Just before Mary became Queen two explorers, Sir Hugh Willoughby and Richard Chancellor, set out with three ships to explore the north-east. Chancellor's ship was separated from the other two in a storm. He and his men landed on the coast of Russia, and made their way on foot to Moscow, where they made a treaty with the ruler, Ivan the Terrible. Meanwhile Willoughby and his men had landed in Lapland, where in the winter they all died of scurvy.

In 1558 Mary died, and her half-sister, Elizabeth, daughter of Ann Boleyn, became Queen. She encouraged English sailors to trade and explore in areas which the Pope had granted to Spain and Portugal. (For details see the table on page 114.) If the Spanish caught them they killed or imprisoned them. Sometimes they made them work as slaves, helping to row the huge Spanish war-galleys. But the English sailors knew that if they avoided capture they could make a fortune.

Date	Name of explorer	Country	Discovery
Before 1400	Unknown	Portugal	Cape Verde Islands ✗
1487	Bartolomew Diaz	Portugal	Cape of Good Hope ✗
1492	Columbus	Spain	West Indies ✗
1498	Vasco da Gama	Portugal	Calicut in India ✓
1499	Alonso de Ojedo	Spain	Venezuela ✓
1500	Pedro Cabal	Portugal	Brazil ✓
1513	Alfonso Albuquerque	Portugal	Canton in China ✓
1519	Ferdinand Magellan (died on voyage)	Spain	Ships sailed round world ✗
1535	Jacques Cartier	France	St Lawrence river in Canada

▲ Voyages by foreign explorers

Study

Opening up the world's trade routes

Portuguese and Spanish explorers, 1492–1519

1 (a) Carefully trace the map on page 100.

(b) The arrows on your map show three important voyages. Two of them are not labelled. With the help of the table above, find out the names of the missing explorers and fill them in.

(c) On your map, find Brazil and Canton. Look at the table of explorers and the key to the map. Then shade in these areas correctly.

2 (a) Read the section headed, 'The Spanish and Portuguese empires' on page 98.

(b) Explain why (i) English merchants did not spend money on voyages of exploration before 1497, (ii) Cabot's discovery of Newfoundland did not encourage them to send out more explorers.

(c) Which English Queen (i) was friendly with Spain and discouraged explorers from going to America, (ii) broke the alliance with Spain and encouraged explorers to go to America?

3 (a) How did the Kings of Spain and Portugal encourage their explorers?

(b) Which country controlled most of the trade with America until 1585?

(c) The actions of (i) the Pope in 1493, (ii) the Catholic Spaniards between 1558 and 1585, made many English merchants and seamen side with the Protestants. Explain why.

out of 20

▶ Spanish and Portuguese voyages of discovery

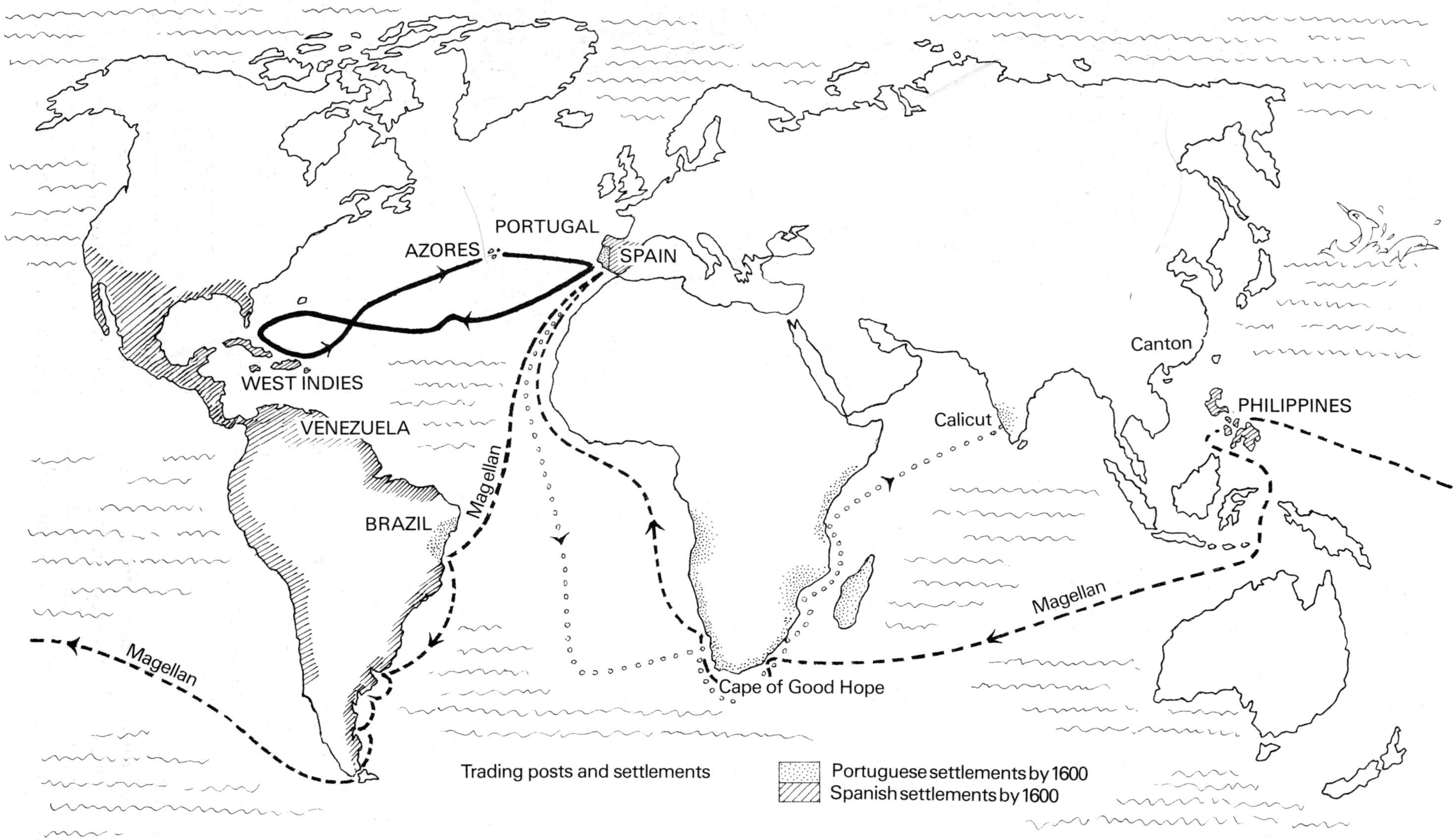

PHILIPPINES

Canton

Calicut

Magellan

Cape of Good Hope

PORTUGAL

SPAIN

AZORES

WEST INDIES

VENEZUELA

BRAZIL

Magellan

Magellan

Magellan

Portuguese settlements by 1600

Spanish settlements by 1600

Trading posts and settlements

Drake defies the Spanish

Drake sets sail for south America

The most famous voyage made by an Englishman in the reign of Queen Elizabeth began at Plymouth on 13 December 1577 when Francis Drake set sail with five ships and 164 men. To deceive the Spaniards he said he was going to Alexandria in the Mediterranean, but in fact he was bound for south America to see if there were any suitable places to establish colonies. He also intended to raid Spanish settlements and rob Spanish cargo ships.

Many important people lent Drake money to hire ships, pay the crews and buy provisions for the voyage. They included the Queen and three courtiers, the Earl of Leicester, Sir Francis Walsingham and Sir Christopher Hatton. They knew that Drake's ships might perish in a storm or be sunk by the Spaniards. They knew that the crews might die of starvation or disease. If this happened they would lose their money. But if Drake returned with a cargo of gold and spices they would make a huge profit.

Drake's ships were very small. The *Pelican*, was 100 tonnes, the *Elizabeth* 80, the *Swan* 50, the *Marigold* 30, and the *Christopher* 15.

Drake's adventures off the African coast

For the first twelve days Drake's ships sailed south past France and Spain and then along the African coast. He was on the lookout for Spanish and Portuguese ships to attack, and in the next month he captured three Spanish fishing boats and five Portuguese ships. He took part of the catch from the fishing boats to feed his men, and stole the cargo of wine which one ship was carrying. He also kidnapped one of its crew, Nina da Silva, who knew the coast of south America well, and would be able to act as pilot for the English fleet.

Life on the *Pelican*

Da Silva lived on the *Pelican* with Drake. He admired the ship, which was very strongly built. Drake's cabin, which was lined with oak panels, was furnished with a comfortable bed, a

▼ As well as sailing round the world and helping to defeat the Spanish Armada, Drake made several voyages to the West Indies selling slaves. He died there in 1596

desk full of charts and a table and chair. Drake spent a lot of time in his cabin. He and his nephew, John, were good artists, and made careful drawings of many parts of the coasts they visited. These drawings were intended as guides for sailors who came after them.

Da Silva found Drake vain and quick-tempered. He hated criticism, and had a captain executed for opposing his wishes. But Drake knew his job. He could tell exactly how a ship would react to every change in the wind, and what adjustments he had to make to the sails and rudder to keep it on course. Drake was also brave. He would lead any attack himself, and took great risks to win riches and fame.

Drake reaches south America

On 5 April 1578 Drake sighted Brazil. After weathering a great storm he landed to take on water, and then sailed south. He anchored near the river Plate to take on fresh food and water. The *Swan* and the *Christopher* were so battered that they were no longer seaworthy, so he abandoned them, and took their crews on board the other ships. Then he set sail again.

Drake rounds Cape Horn

On 20 August Drake's ships entered the Straits of Magellan to round Cape Horn. The passage was difficult to find, with many twists and turns. It was winter, with strong winds and continual frost and snow. The clouds were low, but sometimes they parted, and the sailors caught sight of huge snow-covered mountains on both sides of them. At last, on 6 September, they sailed into the Pacific Ocean.

The next day the three ships were struck by a storm of wind and snow. The *Marigold* sank with all its crew. The *Elizabeth* was driven back into the Straits of Magellan, and returned home. Drake went on in his own ship. He had renamed it the *Golden Hind*, in honour of one of his backers, Sir Christopher Hatton, whose family crest was a golden hind.

Drake begins to plunder

As he sailed up the west coast of south America Drake kept a sharp look-out for Spanish ships. Off the coast of Chile an Indian in a canoe told him that there was a Spanish cargo ship at anchor in the port of Santiago. Drake sailed into the harbour, boarded the ship and took £11,000 in gold from her hold. Then his men went into the town and ransacked the houses. They stole everything of value, including silver vessels from the altar of a chapel.

Further north, at Tarapaca, Drake's men landed and stole thirteen bars of silver from a man they found asleep by the roadside. Then they took 400 kilograms of silver from the backs of a string of pack animals. At Arica they discovered over 500 kilograms of silver lying in

▲ A seventeenth-century model ship, thought to be Drake's *Golden Hind*

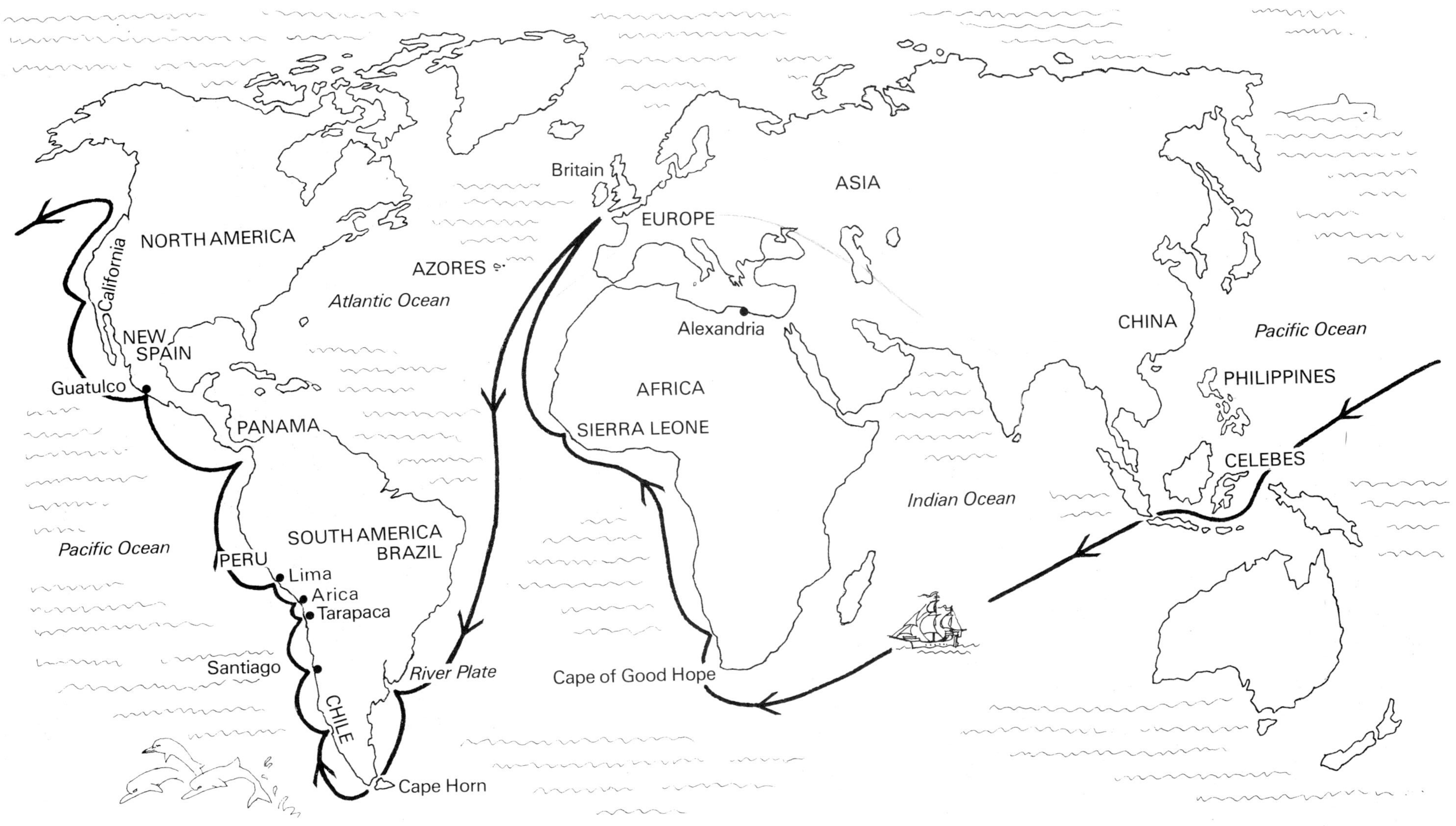

▲ Drake's route round the world

NORTH AMERICA

NEW
SPAIN

California

Guatulco

PANAMA

SOUTH AMERICA
BRAZIL

PERU

Lima

Arica

Tarapaca

Santiago

CHILE

River Plate

Cape Horn

Pacific Ocean

Atlantic Ocean

AZORES

Britain

EUROPE

Alexandria

AFRICA

SIERRA LEONE

Cape of Good Hope

Indian Ocean

ASIA

CHINA

Pacific Ocean

PHILIPPINES

CELEBES

the holds of three unguarded ships at anchor in the harbour, and took it. At Lima there were twelve ships in the harbour when Drake arrived. He searched them and seized a chest full of silver coins and a large quantity of silk and linen.

He seizes a treasure ship

The people at Lima gave Drake some important news. A Spanish treasure ship was in the area, bound for Panama. Drake wasted no time. He cut the cables of the Spanish ships, leaving them to drift helplessly onto the shore. Then he set sail northwards as fast as he could. Seven hundred kilometres south of Panama, Drake caught up with the treasure ship. Its captain refused to surrender, and Drake opened fire, knocking down one mast and damaging another. Then his men boarded the ship and sailed it to a sheltered anchorage. Here they unloaded the treasure and stowed it on board the *Golden Hind*. It took them six days. There were fruit, sugar, thirteen chests of silver coins, 40 kilograms of gold and 26 tonnes of bar silver.

The *Golden Hind* set sail again laden with gold and silver. A few days later Drake came across a ship carrying silk and china. He and his men boarded it. They took some of the cloth and a jewel belonging to the captain—a solid gold falcon with an emerald in its beak. Drake then sailed to the port of Guatulco and sent his men ashore to stretch their legs. They ransacked the town and returned carrying gold, silver and jewellery.

Drake claims a new colony

Drake was now ready to go home, but first his crew beached the ship on a small island. They carefully scraped all the weeds and shells from its hull and greased it so that it would slip easily through the water. Then they set course for the north, hoping to be able to get back to England by sailing round the top of north America.

The days passed, and the *Golden Hind* sailed steadily northwards. It began to grow cold, and there was no sign of any route to the east. So Drake decided to cross the Pacific and make his way home round the Cape of Good Hope. But first he landed on the coast of California to take on food and water, and before he left he nailed a brass plate to a post naming the country 'Nova

Albion', and claiming it in the name of Queen Elizabeth.

Drake sails for home

On 23 July 1579 Drake set out westwards across the Pacific. In the middle of October he sighted the East Indies. He and his men spent five months there, taking on supplies, cleaning the ship, and buying several tonnes of cloves to take back to England. Then they set sail again.

On 8 January 1580 the *Golden Hind* ran aground suddenly on a shallow reef near Celebes. She stuck fast and the crew had to throw three tonnes of cloves, eight cannons and several bags of meal overboard to lighten the ship. At last she floated free. After a couple more calls to take on fresh fruit and water, Drake sailed for home. He rounded the Cape of Good Hope on 18 June, called at Sierra Leone on 22 July, and reached England on 3 November 1580.

Drake's triumphant return

Drake had sailed round the world, and returned to England with his ship loaded down with gold and silver. The Queen received £300,000 as her share of the profits, and everybody else who had lent him money got £47 back for every pound they had lent him. Francis Drake was a hero, and the Queen herself came on board the *Golden Hind* at Deptford and knighted him.

Study

Use your imagination

1 Thomas Barton is the cabin boy on board Drake's ship. His duties are to keep the cabin tidy and to wait on Drake and his officers at mealtimes. Write an account of his voyage round the world with Drake.

Things to write about:

Drake's cabin and the food he and his officers ate.

The voyage through the Straits of Magellan and the renaming of the ship.

A raid that Thomas Barton took part in. *x2 (inc. treasure ship)*

Drake's return home.

(Think of a time when you have helped someone to do an important job.) *Da Silva! (Pg. 101)*

20 marks

2 Write the account of Drake's voyage that da Silva might have given when he returned to Spain and had to explain why he had sailed round the world on an English ship.

▼ Drake used some of the money he made from his voyage round the world to buy Buckland Abbey, near Plymouth, from Sir Richard Grenville, the explorer

Things to write about:

The reason da Silva gave for joining Drake.

One of Drake's raids on Spanish property.

Da Silva's opinion of Drake as a leader.

His reasons for thinking that the English intended to settle in America one day.

(Think of a time when you had to help someone, even though you didn't want to.)

3 Christopher Hatton was one of Elizabeth's courtiers who gave Drake money for his expedition. Write an account of how he helped to plan the expedition and waited anxiously to see if Drake's voyage would be a success.

Things to write about:

A meeting where the courtiers discuss the profit they may make and the risks of the voyage.

Drake's ships sail from Plymouth in 1577.

The *Elizabeth* returns to England, bringing news of gales and stormy seas.

Drake arrives home triumphantly in 1580.

(Think of an important plan that you made with a friend, which you had to rely on him or her to carry out.)

Trouble between England and Spain

Philip II demands compensation

When the Spanish King, Philip II, heard how Drake had plundered Spanish ships and settlements, he was very angry. He ordered the Spanish ambassador in England to demand compensation, but Elizabeth would not listen. She did not trust Philip. She knew that both his father and his mother were descended from Edward III. This gave him a good claim to the English throne. The Pope had declared that Elizabeth had no right to be queen, and she believed that Philip wanted to become King of England and restore the Roman Catholic religion.

At that time Spain ruled Holland and Flanders and kept a large number of soldiers there under the command of the Duke of Parma. Elizabeth feared that these soldiers might be used to invade England, and when the people of Holland rebelled against Spanish rule she sent arms, money and men to help drive the Spaniards out. This made Philip even angrier, and he began to plan an attack on England.

Philip prepares to attack

Philip decided to attack England by sending an *armada* (a fleet of armed ships) up the English Channel to Dunkirk where the Duke of Parma would be waiting with his army. Some of the men would board the ships. The rest would be packed onto barges. Then the whole force would sail across the Channel and land on the English coast.

In 1582 Philip began to prepare. He sent extra troops to Parma and paid for new ships to be built and old ones repaired. His advisers urged him to hurry, but Philip was not so sure. He knew it would be difficult and expensive to invade England. In addition, though he had quite a good claim to the English throne, he knew that Mary Stuart, Queen of Scots, had a much better claim, and as long as she was alive he hesitated. 'In so great a matter,' he said, 'it is better to walk with leaden feet.'

▼ Philip II worked hard. He spent many hours reading reports from his ministers and ambassadors, and wrote long and detailed instructions to them

In 1567 the Scottish Protestants had rebelled against Queen Mary, and she had fled to England to ask Elizabeth for help. Elizabeth was her second cousin, and Mary took it for granted that she would do her best to help. But Elizabeth did not trust Mary and imprisoned her. In 1586 Mary was accused of plotting from her prison in Derbyshire to have Elizabeth murdered. She was tried and found guilty. On 8 February 1587 she was executed. When Philip heard the news in Spain at the end of March he did not hesitate any longer. He wrote to the Marquis of Santa Cruz, the commander of his fleet, telling him he must be ready to sail for England by the summer.

Study

Philip, Elizabeth and Mary

King Philip of Spain. Spanish men wore black clothes. Their doublets were shaped like a soldier's breastplate

Elizabeth of England. Before about 1577 the English were friendly with the Spanish and copied Spanish fashions

Mary, Queen of Scots. The Scots were allies of the French and copied French fashions

1 Rewrite the list below in the order in which the events happened:

Philip plans to invade England, using troops stationed in Flanders.

Drake raids Spanish colonies and ships.

Mary, Queen of Scots, is executed and the Spanish fleet prepares to sail for England.

Elizabeth refuses to pay compensation to Spain and helps the Dutch rebels against Philip.

Philip orders his ambassador in England to demand compensation for the damage done by Drake.

2 (a) List three reasons why Elizabeth feared Philip.

(b) What crime against Elizabeth was Mary accused of, and what happened to her when she was found guilty?

3 (a) In what year did Philip begin the preparations to invade England?

(b) Give two or more reasons why he delayed putting his plan into action.

England and Spain at war

Elizabeth sends Drake to attack the Spaniards

In England, Elizabeth and her Council soon heard that Philip was preparing to attack. The navy needed more time to prepare its ships and obtain supplies of food, gunpowder and ammunition to defend the country. So the Council ordered Sir Francis Drake to sail to Spain and try to delay the Armada.

Drake set sail with a force of 26 ships and at the end of April 1587 he reached the Spanish port of Cadiz. Here he found 60 ships at anchor. He destroyed or captured 37 of them.

Drake left Cadiz and sailed west to Cape St Vincent, where he stayed until the end of May. His fleet spent the time roaming up and down the coast attacking all the merchant ships they saw. Many were bound for Lisbon, laden with seasoned wooden staves for making barrels. Ships used barrels to carry water, meat, fish and flour. Drake guessed that the barrel staves were on their way to Santa Cruz's fleet, and ordered them to be burnt so that the Spanish would have to use green unseasoned wood to make the casks for their fleet. These casks would leak, split and rot, and the provisions they contained would spoil.

In all Drake destroyed 1,700 tonnes of staves. It was a huge quantity, and Drake realised that the Spaniards must have a very large fleet preparing to attack England. He wrote home to the Queen's Council with a warning. 'The like preparation was never heard of nor known as the King of Spain ... daily maketh to invade England. Look well to the coast of Sussex.'

Drake captures a merchant ship

On 1 June Drake sailed for home. On his way he captured a Spanish merchant ship loaded with pepper, cinnamon, cloves, calico, silk, ivory, gold, silver and gems, worth £114,000. His share of this amounted to £17,000. Drake was pleased with his voyage. 'I have singed the King of Spain's beard,' he said when he arrived back in England.

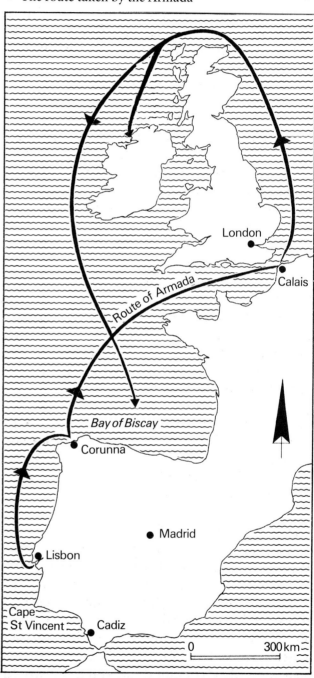

▼ The route taken by the Armada

Philip orders the Armada to sail in 1588

Back in Spain Philip II realised that his fleet would not now be ready until 1588. So he wrote to Santa Cruz ordering him to be ready to sail for England by the middle of February. 'Success depends mostly upon speed,' Philip told him. 'Be quick.' But Santa Cruz was ill, and on 9 February he died. Philip appointed the Duke of Medina Sidonia to take his place.

Medina Sidonia did not want the job. He wrote to Philip saying, 'I am always seasick and always catch cold. Since I have no experience either of the sea or of war, I cannot feel I ought to command so important an enterprise.' But Philip knew that Medina Sidonia was honest, steady and brave. So he insisted. Eventually the duke gave way, and went to the port of Lisbon to take command of the fleet.

Medina Sidonia takes command and sets sail

At Lisbon, Medina Sidonia found that, for months past, supplies for the fleet had been flowing into the port. But Santa Cruz had been too ill to control where they were put. So some ships were overloaded with food, but had no powder and shot, while others had plenty of ammunition but no food. Some had no troops on board. Others were overcrowded.

It took Medina Sidonia three months to sort it all out, but on 9 May the Armada of 130 ships was at last ready and set sail. It carried about 22,000 men, and a vast quantity of arms and ammunition, including 123,790 cannon balls. Almost at once a gale blew up and trapped the fleet in the river Tagus for nearly three weeks. But on 28 May the ships set sail again. The weather was bad. They had hoped for a steady breeze. Instead there were long periods of flat calm when the sails hung limp on the masts, and sudden unexpected storms which scattered the fleet in all directions.

The Armada puts into Corunna

By 19 June the fleet had reached Corunna, and Medina Sidonia called his captains together for a conference. He was upset by what he heard. Some ships had sprung leaks in the storms, and almost all the captains reported that their provisions were rotting and their drinking water turning foul. As a result many of their men were ill. The duke decided that he would not sail on to England until these things had been put right, so he anchored in Corunna harbour for a month while his ships were repaired, fresh provisions were taken on board and the sick men recovered.

The Armada enters the Channel and is sighted

On 21 July Medina Sidonia set sail again. At last there was a steady wind from the south which blew the Armada towards the mouth of the English Channel. They made good time, and on Saturday 30 July they entered the Channel.

As soon as lookouts on the shore in Cornwall sighted the Spanish fleet, they lit a beacon of wood and tar on a nearby hilltop. A few miles away, on the next beacon hill, other watchers saw the smoke and lit their own beacon fire. In this way the news was spread, and by evening people all over England knew that the Spanish fleet had been sighted.

At the same time a message was sent to Plymouth where the English fleet, commanded by Lord Howard of Effingham, was lying at anchor. The message reached Howard when the tide was coming in, and the wind was

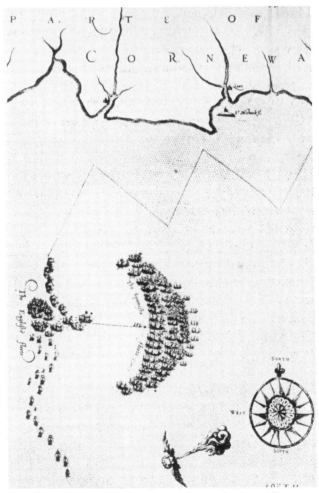

▲ This map, engraved in 1590, shows the Spanish Armada sailing in its crescent formation up the Channel. The English fleet is following

▼ A picture painted at the time by an unknown artist showing the fireships sailing into the Spanish fleet at Calais

blowing straight into the harbour mouth. Howard had to wait six hours until the tide turned before he could get any of his ships out of harbour. Then he set sail.

The Spanish formation

Meanwhile the Spanish fleet sailed on up the Channel. The ships kept close together in a crescent formation. In the middle were the cargo boats and troop ships. The fighting galleons sailed at the sides, making the horns of the crescent, to protect other ships from attack.

Medina Sidonia had very few long-range guns, so if English ships attacked his fleet he wanted to lure them in close. Then he could bombard them with his heavy cannons, sail alongside them, board them and capture them.

Howard's plan of attack

Howard of Effingham had quite different ideas. His best ships were faster and easier to handle than the Spanish boats. He also had more long-range cannons. So he decided to sail up and down bombarding the Spanish fleet from a distance, and pouncing on any ship that drifted away from the main fleet.

Howard's tactics did not work. He found that many of the cannon balls did not fit the guns properly, and some of the gunpowder was of poor quality. So at long range the cannons were very inaccurate, and most shots splashed harmlessly into the water. Howard also found that the Spanish were much better sailors than he had expected, and kept their tight formation.

Occasionally a ship would fall back. Immediately two or three English ships sailed up to it, firing their cannons. As soon as the English came within range the Spanish gunners opened fire. At the same time the crew hoisted more sails, and the ship began to catch up with the rest of the Armada, drawing the English boats closer and closer to the main Spanish fleet. It was a trap, and when they realised what was happening the English ships turned away, leaving the great Armada to sail on.

The Armada at Calais

On 6 August Medina Sidonia reached Calais. He anchored off the coast, and sent a message to the Duke of Parma asking him when his troops would be ready to cross to England. When the English commanders saw the Spanish ships lying at anchor they realised that their chance had come. They chose eight of their ships, and ordered the crews to transfer all the supplies on them to other vessels. Then they filled them with wood, oil, tar and anything else that would burn easily. They packed gunpowder into the cannons, and rammed two cannon balls into each. As darkness fell they hoisted the sails of the eight vessels and lashed the rudders in place. Then they set fire to the contents of the ships, and let the wind and tide carry them into the Spanish fleet.

▼ Queen Elizabeth ordered this medal to be struck after the defeat of the Armada. The inscription means 'God breathed and they were scattered'

Sailors in wooden ships always fear fire, and when the Spanish seamen saw eight blazing ships coming at them out of the night they panicked. They cut their anchor cables, hoisted their sails and set out to sea to avoid the fireships whose guns, heated red-hot, fired glowing cannon balls into the air. When day dawned the Spanish Armada had scattered.

The fight in the North Sea

Howard sent the English to attack the scattered Spanish fleet. Many of the Spanish fought bravely, but they were running short of powder and shot. So the English were able to close in, and firing at point-blank range, their guns holed and weakened the wooden hulls of many of the enemy ships. And all the time a steady south wind was blowing the Armada up into the North Sea, away from Dunkirk and the waiting Spanish troops.

Gradually the wind freshened, until it was blowing a full gale. Howard ordered the English ships to sail back into port, leaving the Spanish fleet to the mercy of the wind and the sea. But he did not think the fight was over. He knew that if the wind changed Medina Sidonia might still reach Dunkirk and pick up Parma's men. 'Their force is wonderful great and strong,' he wrote in a report to the Council.

Queen Elizabeth at Tilbury

On shore soldiers were preparing to fight against the Spanish troops if they landed. Some were waiting at Tilbury to repel any attack on London, and on 18 August the Queen herself came to inspect them. On 19 August she addressed her troops:

> 'I am come amongst you not for my recreation and disport, but being resolved, in the midst and heat of the battle, to live or die amongst you all ... I know I have the body of a weak and feeble woman, but I have the heart and stomach of a king, and of a King of England too, and think foul scorn that Parma, or Spain, or any prince of Europe should dare to invade the borders of my realm to which, rather than dishonour shall grow by me, I myself will take up arms.'

The Armada makes for home

In fact, the Armada did not turn back. The southerly gale blew the Spanish ships further and further north. Four of their biggest ships, which had been damaged in the fight, sank. The rest made their way round the north of Scotland, and then turned south for Spain. Their voyage was a nightmare. They ran short of provisions, and their water casks had warped and leaked. Many of the men fell ill, and all were weak from lack of food. They had not the strength to sail the ships properly, and when gales blew they simply ran before the wind and hoped for the best. Many were wrecked off the coasts of Scotland and Ireland. In the end only 67 returned safely to Spain. Philip's great plan to invade England had failed.

Study

The Armada sails against England

1 Rewrite the list below in the correct chronological order.

 The Armada is delayed at Corunna.

 The English light beacons to warn everyone that the Armada has entered the Channel.

 Drake raids the Spanish fleet in Cadiz harbour.

 English ships follow the Armada along the Channel.

 English fire-ships sail into Calais harbour and scatter the Spaniards.

 Santa Cruz dies and Medina Sidonia takes command of the Armada.

2 (a) Divide a double page into four sections. Draw one of the heads below in each section.

(b) Copy the two descriptions under the correct drawings:

Commander of Spanish Armada
Set out with 130 ships
Failed to invade England
Returned with 67 ships

Was ordered to delay the Armada
Raided Cadiz and sunk Spanish ships
Warned Elizabeth to guard the coast of Sussex

(c) Write brief notes under the two remaining drawings.

3 (a) Copy the words inscribed on the Armada medal, shown on page 111.

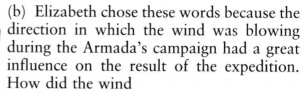

(b) Elizabeth chose these words because the direction in which the wind was blowing during the Armada's campaign had a great influence on the result of the expedition. How did the wind

 (i) Prevent the English from stopping the Spaniards sailing along the Channel,

 (ii) Help the English to scatter the Spanish ships in Calais harbour,

 (iii) Prevent the Armada from picking up the Spanish troops at Dunkirk?

Discussion

(a) Did Philip have good reasons for going to war with England in 1588? In pairs, consider:

 Drake's raids on the Spanish colonies and Elizabeth's refusal to punish him,

 The Pope's declaration that Elizabeth had no right to be Queen of England,

 The help the English were giving to the rebels against Spain in the Netherlands,

 Anything else you think is important.

(b) Decide whether or not you think that, from Philip's point of view, he was justified in going to war with England. Give reasons for your answer.

(c) Choose one person who thinks that Philip had a good case, and one who does not, to read their answers to the class. What do the rest of you think?

Sir Francis Drake

The Marquis of Santa Cruz

The Duke of Medina Sidonia

Lord Howard

The beginning of England's empire

During the Middle Ages England had tried to establish an empire in Europe. After the Armada, she no longer bothered. It was easier and cheaper to do as Spain and Portugal had done and set up colonies in America or the Indies.

So English colonists sailed to north America. Gradually they established a string of colonies along the east coast. These were not as rich as the Spanish colonies, but they provided England with valuable supplies of tobacco, fish, timber and furs.

Some English merchants thought they could make fortunes trading in the East. In 1600 a number of them formed the *Company of merchants of London trading to the East Indies*. Queen Elizabeth gave them a charter, and eventually the East India Company grew into the richest and most powerful trading company in the world and brought enormous wealth to Britain.

The importance of sea power
England had to be able to protect her colonies and merchant ships from attack by other countries. This needed a large, efficient navy.

▲ A portrait of Queen Elizabeth, painted after the defeat of the Armada. Her right hand, resting on the globe, covers north America

In the seventeenth century, the Dutch were England's chief trading rivals. By 1609 they had driven the Spanish out of their country, and they used their ships to carry goods all over the world. They wanted to trade everywhere, including England and her colonies. This upset English merchants who were determined to make as much money as they could out of their country's new possessions. They wanted to be the only people allowed to trade with the English colonies. As a result, the two countries quarrelled.

Date	Name of explorer	Achievement
1497	John Cabot	Discovered Newfoundland
1553	Hugh Willoughby Richard Chancellor	Discovered a route to northern Russia
1577	Francis Drake	Voyage round world
1585	Walter Raleigh	Founded a colony in Virginia
1620	Pilgrim Fathers	Settled in New England

▲ Voyages by British explorers

Study

The English overseas

Copy the map opposite.

1 Copy the sentences below, using these words to fill in the gaps correctly:

> possessions   overseas   Dutch
> London   Indies   America

After the Armada, the English found it was easier to build up an empire _____ than in Europe. English settlers set up colonies in _____ and in 1600 a company was set up in _____ to trade with the _____. The English merchants wanted to make as much money as they could from England's new _____ and would not let the _____ trade with the English colonies.

2 (a) List the goods that the English imported from their American colonies.

(b) Why did the London merchants form the East India Company?

3 (a) Why, after 1609, were the Dutch able to concentrate on building up their trade overseas?

(b) Copy the sentence below that you think is correct:

> The English in the seventeenth century were more generous than the Spaniards in the sixteenth century because they allowed the Dutch to trade with English colonies overseas.

> The English in the seventeenth century, like the Spaniards in the sixteenth century, would not allow foreigners to trade with their colonies overseas.

114

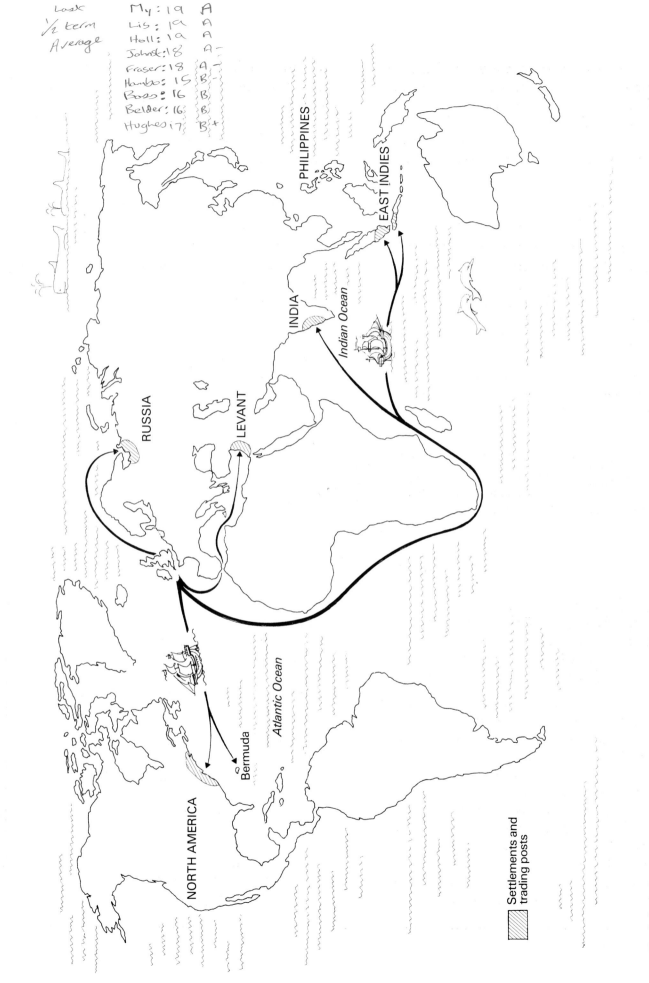

PHILIPPINES

EAST INDIES

INDIA

Indian Ocean

RUSSIA

LEVANT

NORTH AMERICA

Bermuda

Atlantic Ocean

Settlements and
trading posts

▲ English settlements and trading posts in about 1620

Further work

Writing

1 (a) Choose four or more pieces of information to include in a paragraph on:

Life on board ship in the sixteenth century.

List your information in brief notes. For example, your first note might read:

Most ships—small, crowded.

(b) Write the paragraph, turning your notes into interesting sentences.

2 (a) Choose four or more pieces of information to include in a paragraph on each of the following:

English seamen before the Armada.

The English overseas after the Armada.

List your information in brief notes. For example, your first note might read:

1497 Cabot discovered Newfoundland for H VII.

(b) Write your paragraphs, turning your notes into interesting sentences.

3 (a) Make a list of three paragraph headings for an essay on:

The New World in the sixteenth century.

For example, your first heading might be:

Columbus in the West Indies.

(b) Make a list of brief notes under each heading.

(c) Write your essay, turning your notes into interesting sentences.

Drawing

1 There is a story that a map-maker drew an island that did not exist on one of his maps in order to please his wife, who wanted her own island.

(a) Draw a map of an island that you would have liked to discover. Include:

the main points of the compass,
the scale of your map,
mountains and rivers,
a harbour,
the main settlement,
paths across the island.

(b) Give your island a name and say in which ocean it is to be found.

2 (a) Copy the map of Drake's voyage round the world on page 103.

(b) Maps often had pictures on them, showing, for example, buildings, people and battles at sea. Choose four or more incidents from Drake's voyage round the world and draw pictures to illustrate them in the correct place on your map.

3 (a) Copy the map of the Armada's route on page 109.

(b) Look at the annotated map on page 75. Then annotate your map by writing brief notes on the events at:

Lisbon   Corunna   Plymouth
Calais   Tilbury

Mime: a shipwreck

In groups of six

Imagine that you are on a ship at sea that has been caught in a violent storm. The captain is shouting orders to his crew through cupped hands. His men are lowering the sails and throwing baggage overboard to lighten the ship. The gentlemen on board are getting in the way. The ship begins to break up...

(a) Divide into equal groups of gentlemen and seamen.

(b) Prepare a scene, to last about two minutes, miming the shipwreck.

(c) Choose two or three groups to perform their scenes to the class.

Quiz: Where did it happen?

Where did the following events take place?

John Cabot set sail for America.

Drake stole the ornaments from a church.

English fire-ships scattered the Spanish Armada.

Make up your own 'Where did it happen?' quiz.

Library work

Look up *Mary, Queen of Scots* under the letter M in an encyclopedia or in a history book on the sixteenth century. Mary was married three times. Who were her three husbands and how did each of them die?

6 The London of Samuel Pepys

The Fire of London

The Fire breaks out

It was three o'clock in the morning on Sunday 2 September 1666. It had been a hot, dry summer in London, and a strong wind was blowing through the city streets. At a house in Seething Lane near the Tower of London, a number of maids were at work preparing for a dinner party which their master, Samuel Pepys, was giving later in the day.

One of the maids, named Jane, looked out and saw a red flickering glow in the sky. Somewhere in London some houses were on fire. Jane thought it seemed a big fire, and decided to wake Pepys. He got up and looked out. He thought the fire was a long way away, went back to bed and soon fell asleep again.

At 7 a.m. Pepys woke. In the daylight the fire seemed much smaller and further away, so he dressed and began to tidy his room. Jane interrupted him. She had heard that 300 houses had burnt down, and that the whole of Fish Street just by London Bridge was now on fire.

Pepys goes to see the Fire

Pepys decided to go to see for himself. First he went to the Tower where he could get a good view. He was horrified to see a huge fire blazing round the end of London Bridge.

To get a closer look he went to the river and hired a boat which carried him opposite to where the fire was raging. Pepys was appalled by what he saw. Everything was tinder dry, and the flames destroyed the wooden houses in minutes, while even the stone steeple of the church of St Lawrence Poultney seemed to be blazing from top to bottom. Nobody was bothering to put the fire out. Instead people were carrying goods out of the houses and dumping them in boats at the riverside.

Pepys goes to the King

After watching the scene for an hour, Pepys hurried to Whitehall palace where he told Charles II and his brother the Duke of York what he had seen. Charles ordered him to go

▲ A Dutch print showing the Fire of London. St Paul's Cathedral is in the centre. London Bridge is on the right. Seething Lane, where Pepys lived, was just behind the Tower on the right

117

▼ A hand syringe, which held about 4 litres of water. At the time of the Fire, it was the only kind of fire-fighting equipment available

back, find the Lord Mayor, and tell him to pull down houses to make gaps to stop the fire spreading further.

Pepys pushed his way through the streets, which were crowded with people carrying their possessions away from the fire. At last, in Canning Street, he found the Lord Mayor, Sir Thomas Bludworth. The mayor had been up all night, and when he heard the King's orders he said he could do nothing. 'I am spent,' he gasped, 'people will not obey me. I have been pulling down houses, but the fire overtakes us faster than we can do it.' And he went home for some food and rest.

The Fire spreads faster

Pepys too went home. It was nearly noon, and time for his dinner party. At the meal he and his guests talked of nothing but the fire, and as soon as they had finished Pepys went out again. He wandered through the streets, noticing that as the fire spread, blown by the strong wind, people were having to move their goods for a second or even a third time to keep them safe.

Pepys took a boat on the river but he was frightened by the sparks falling on him. So he went to an ale house and sat drinking. As it grew dark the fire seemed like a great arch of flame, 'the churches, houses and all on fire and flaming. And a horrid noise the flames made, and the crackling of houses', as they burnt.

Pepys went home with a sad heart, and found one of his clerks, Tom Hayter, there. Tom's house had burnt down, and he had escaped with a few possessions. Pepys promised him a bed, and took in his goods.

Pepys moves his possessions

Soon Pepys grew very worried about his own house, for the flames were creeping closer and closer. So he, his wife and his servants loaded all his gold coin, jewellery and papers into a cart, and Pepys drove it to a friend's house in Bethnal Green. They carried the rest of his possessions down to the river, and loaded them onto a boat. This took them all night and most of the next day. In the evening they ate the cold remains of Sunday's dinner and slept on the floor.

The Fire comes closer

By Tuesday the fire was burning 'with great fury' in Tower Street, only 200 metres away. Pepys dug a hole in his garden, and hid his wine and Parmesan cheese in it. He wrote a letter to his father, but found that the Post Office had burnt down, so he could not send it.

In the evening he sent out to a local cook's shop for a roast shoulder of mutton, which he and his wife ate in their empty house. Later he went out into the garden. The sky, he said, was 'all on fire' all round them.

In Tower Street men were busy blowing up houses with gunpowder. This left gaps which the fire could not cross. But there was not enough gunpowder to blow up all the houses in the path of the fire, and it continued to spread.

That night Pepys, 'mighty weary', and with feet so sore that he was hardly able to stand, again lay down to sleep on the floor. But at two o'clock in the morning his wife woke him with news that the church at the end of their street was on fire. Pepys decided it was time to take his wife to a safe place, so he got up, went with her to the riverside and took a boat to Woolwich, where he left her at a friend's house.

The Fire dies down

Pepys returned, fully expecting to find his house on fire. But the wind had dropped just in time, and the fire had stopped spreading. His house was safe. Slowly the fire burnt itself out. It left more than three-quarters of the old city in ashes. More than 13,000 houses had burnt down, as well as 85 churches, including St Paul's Cathedral. London was, said Pepys, 'the saddest sight of desolation that I ever saw'.

Studying the story

How do we know?

Pepys's diary

Pepys was born on 23 February 1633 in Salisbury Court just off Fleet Street. His father was a tailor. The Pepys family came from Cambridgeshire and were related by marriage to Henry Montagu, Earl of Manchester. When Charles II became King, Edward Montagu, Henry's relative, used his influence with him to get Pepys a good job, working for the government.

Pepys often went to the King's palace at Whitehall. He felt that he was living at the centre of events at an important time, so he decided to note down everything interesting that he did or heard each day, and to write up his notes in the form of a diary. He started to do this in 1660 and kept it up until 1669 when his eyes became too weak for him to continue. Today, when we read his account of the Fire of London, it seems as if he is telling us about something that happened yesterday.

▶ Pepys always used shorthand in his diary. This photograph shows part of the first page of his diary.

1 (a) Why did Pepys,
    (i) decide to begin a diary in 1660,
    (ii) stop keeping a diary in 1669?
  (b) Give an example of an important event that he wrote about in his diary.
2 Look at the story of the Fire.
  (a) Name two important people whom Pepys spoke to during the Fire.
  (b) Give two examples of ordinary people whom Pepys saw going about their usual business.
3 (a) Give an example of something that Pepys did to get a better view of the Fire.

  (b) The Fire of London lasted from Sunday 2 September to Wednesday 5 September. Was Pepys in London
    all of that time,
    most of that time,
    a small part of that time?

What do you think?

Consider Pepys's reason for keeping a diary and what he tells us about his movements during the Fire. Would you expect him to have left us a reliable account of what happened? Give reasons for your answer.

→

▲ Wren's monument in about 1800. Today it is surrounded by modern buildings

Wren's Monument

We think that the Fire of London broke out in a bakery in Pudding Lane, just north of London Bridge. Sir Christopher Wren designed the Monument that you can see in the picture to mark the place where the Fire began, and his workmen built it between 1671 and 1677. It is about 73 metres high, and stands about 73 metres from the spot where the bakery was. One of the carvings at its base shows King Charles urging an architect and his masons to set to work and rebuild the ruined city.

Wren's churches

Inside Wren's Monument there are 311 steps leading to the top. From there you can look east to the Tower of London and west to the great dome of St Paul's Cathedral. All the streets between these two buildings were destroyed by the Fire in 1666. Beyond St Paul's you can see the tower of St Bride's in Fleet Street, where the Fire was finally checked.

When you walk through the City of London today you can still see St Paul's Cathedral—the new building Wren designed to replace the one that was burnt down in 1666. You will also find a number of churches that have columns and arches shaped rather like those you would see in a Greek or Roman temple. Most of them were built after about 1670 when the workmen had cleared away the gutted shells of the churches that had once stood there, and are also the work of Sir Christopher Wren.

---

1 (a) When was Wren's Monument built? 1671 - 1677
  (b) Which bridge is it near?
  (c) What did Jane tell Pepys about the area near this bridge on the morning of 2 September 1666?

What do you think?
Does it seem certain that the Fire broke out near London Bridge? Give reasons for your answer.

2 (a) Which church in Fleet Street marks the place in the west of the city where the Fire was checked?

(b) Look at the map on page 121. Which church in Seething Lane marks the place where the Fire ended in the east of London?
(●) How might you recognise a church that Wren designed that was built in the area between these two older churches?

What do you think?
Does the evidence from old and newer churches in the City of London support what Pepys tells us about the area that was destroyed by the Fire? Give reasons for your answer.

Understanding what happened

1 (a) Divide a page into sections, as shown in the time-chart opposite, and copy the chart:

(b) Fill in these notes in the correct place on your time-chart:

Pepys and his wife sleep on the floor of their empty house.

Pepys and his wife pack their belongings.

Pepys takes his wife to Woolwich and returns to find their house is safe.

Pepys takes his valuables to Bethnal Green.

(c) What saved Pepys's house from being burnt down?

2 (a) What orders did the King give to try to check the Fire?

(b) Why were the following people unable to carry out the King's orders completely?

The Lord Mayor

The men in Tower Street

(c) How many buildings were destroyed by the Fire?

3 (a) Why was it difficult for Pepys to get from Whitehall to Canning Street?

(b) Why did Tom Hayter come to Pepys?

(c) Name two kinds of transport that Pepys used to move his belongings to safety.

The four worst days of the Fire	
Day	The Fire
Sunday 2 Sept.	The Fire begins
Monday 3 Sept.	The Fire spreads
Tuesday 4 Sept.	The Fire reaches Tower Street
Wednesday 5 Sept.	The Fire reaches Seething Lane

▼ Buildings in the shaded area were destroyed by the Fire. Tuesday, 4 September 1666, was the day when most houses were burnt. Notice how the Fire stopped just short of All Hallows' Church in Seething Lane

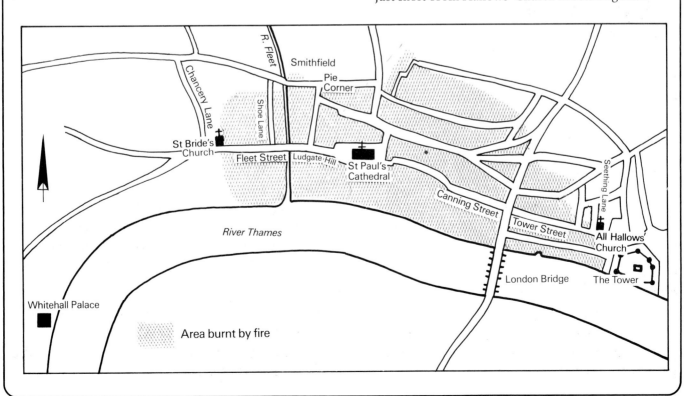

Area burnt by fire

Further work

Writing

1 (a) Write four entries for a diary, covering the worst days of the Fire, that might have been written by any one of the following people:

        Mrs Pepys   Tom Hayter
        the Lord Mayor of London

2 Write the letter that Pepys might have tried to send to his father on Tuesday, 4 September 1666. You might mention:

the damage the Fire has done so far,

what you have done to protect your belongings,

what you will do if the Fire gets any nearer to your home.

3 Write a report on the Fire of London for Charles II. Say what caused the Fire to spread so rapidly and make suggestions for preventing fires on this scale in the future: You might consider:

the materials that the houses were made of,

the weather conditions,

available supplies of gunpowder and fire-fighting equipment.

Drawing

1 Look at the picture of London on page 117. Then draw your idea of what the Fire looked like as seen from a boat on the Thames.

2 Copy the map of London on page 121 into your book, leaving room around it to make notes.

Annotate your map to show what happened at four of the places mentioned in the story of the Fire.

3 Draw a set of three pictures to illustrate a modern edition of Pepys's diary of the Fire.

Drama

In groups of four, write a scene with Pepys, Mrs Pepys and two of the guests at their dinner party at Seething Lane on Sunday, 2 September. The guests live at Bethnal Green and their home is not in danger. Pepys tells them what he has seen that morning. Mrs Pepys is worried that the fire will spread to Seething Lane if the wind does not change. The guests offer to help.

Give everyone at least two things each to say. When you have written and rehearsed your scenes, choose two groups to perform their work in front of the class.

Britain in the reign of Charles I

England and Scotland

When Pepys was born Charles I was King. Charles came from Scotland. His father, King James VI of Scotland, was Queen Elizabeth's second cousin, and had become King James I of England when Elizabeth died. The two kingdoms have been united ever since.

Charles I, who became King in 1625, believed that his power as King came from God. He thought his subjects ought to obey all his orders, and make sure that he had enough money to rule the country as he thought best.

Charles was also a great supporter of the Church of England. The Church was ruled by bishops, whom he appointed, and all its clergy had to follow the service in the Prayer Book.

The English Parliament

Many Members of Parliament disagreed with Charles. They thought the King ought to take their advice on how to rule the country, and they believed that they had the right to refuse to grant him money if he took no notice of what they said.

They also believed that the Church needed to be reformed. They did not want bishops to rule the Church. They thought that people ought to be able to elect their own clergymen. They also objected to the services in the Prayer Book. They thought the form of the service ought to depend on how the congregation felt, and not be laid down in a book. These critics of the Church were known as Puritans.

▲ These three portraits of Charles I were painted by his court painter, Sir Anthony Van Dyck, for an Italian sculptor who made a bust of Charles

Charles dissolves Parliament

Charles thought that Parliament had no right to criticise him, his ministers, or the Church. When Parliament refused to grant him any money unless he did as it wished he grew very angry, and in 1629 he decided to rule without Parliament. He continued to collect taxes even though Parliament had not granted them.

Charles's chief minister at this time was Thomas Wentworth, Earl of Strafford. He was hard and ruthless. He believed that the King ought to try to frighten his opponents by arresting and punishing their leaders.

Politics and pamphlets in London

Londoners took a great interest in politics. The King and his advisers lived and worked in Whitehall palace, and many Londoners either knew them by sight, or had heard stories about them from people who worked in or around the royal palace. A French visitor to London noticed that if a courtier hired a boat on the Thames the boatman immediately began to question him about politics as he rowed along, and was not afraid to give his opinion.

Most Londoners were opposed to Charles. There were secret printing presses in the capital which published pamphlets attacking the royal family and the Church of England. In 1637

three authors of such pamphlets were arrested and tried. One, William Prynne, was a lawyer. He had criticised the Queen for dancing and going to the theatre, and had also attacked the bishops. Henry Burton, a London clergyman, had described the bishops as 'upstart mushrumps,' while John Bastwick, a doctor, had written that most Church of England clergymen were 'proud, ungrateful, idle, wicked and illiterate asses'.

The King's court sentenced the three men to stand in the pillory and have their ears cut off, fined them £5,000 each and imprisoned them for life. As a rule only beggars and cheats were made to stand in the pillory. Judges usually treated doctors, lawyers and clergymen with more respect.

Charles and Strafford believed that this severe and humiliating punishment would frighten their enemies, but it only made Londoners hate the King and his ministers more than ever. When the three men were brought out to the pillory they were cheered by a large crowd and people strewed sweet herbs at their feet and offered them wine to drink. All three made speeches to the crowd, and when their ears had been cut off, people pressed so close round them to dip their handkerchiefs in the blood to keep as a souvenir that Burton fainted.

Who should govern the Church and State?

The Puritan Churches

MINISTER

ELDERS   Chosen from the Church Officials

Appointed by the Elders

CHURCH OFFICIALS (PRESBYTERS)   Chosen by the Congregation

CONGREGATION OF ORDINARY PEOPLE

13(a) Copy the two diagrams.
(b) One diagram shows how the King wanted the Church to be governed. The other shows how many Members of Parliament wanted the Church to be governed. Write a sentence under each diagram, saying which is which.

The Church of England

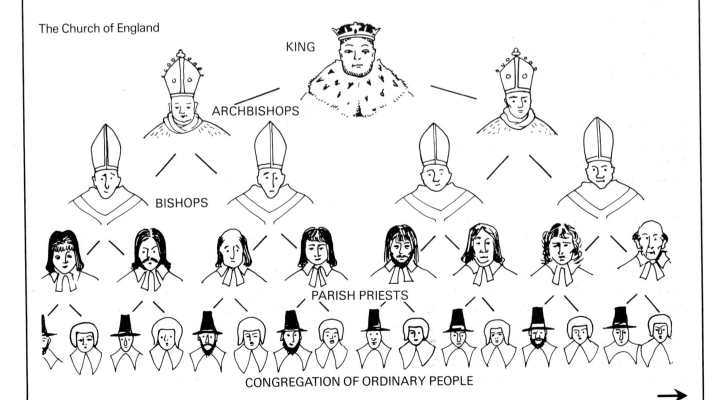

KING

ARCHBISHOPS

BISHOPS

PARISH PRIESTS

CONGREGATION OF ORDINARY PEOPLE

→

2 (a) Start a new page in your book and count down five lines. Then copy these statements, starting each one on a new line:

The King should rule with the help of his Parliament.

If he does not take Parliament's advice, Parliament should not give him any money.

(b) Turn your page into a pamphlet that might have been written by a Puritan in about 1630 by adding two or more other complaints that a pamphleteer might have made against the King.

(c) Give your pamphlet a heading that will attract attention.

3 (a) Look at the picture of Lilburne being flogged 'at a cart's tail' on page 124. Write the description of the scene that might have been given by someone in the street who saw Lilburne being punished.

(b) Whom did Strafford advise the King to punish in order to stop people opposing the government?

(c) How did pamphleteers like John Lilburne manage to spread their views among the Londoners?

The Civil War and Cromwell

Charles calls Parliament

As long as Parliament did not meet, there was nothing Charles's opponents could do. But in 1638 a rebellion broke out in Scotland. Charles needed money to pay an army to defeat the Scots. He called Parliament, believing that the members would grant him money to pay his troops. But he found that they would not give him anything until they had passed laws making it impossible for him to rule without Parliament, and had punished his ministers.

The trial and execution of Strafford

Most Members of Parliament hated and feared Strafford, and in 1641 they passed an Act that declared him guilty of high treason, and sentenced him to be beheaded.

But before Strafford could be executed the King had to give his consent. Charles had already written to Strafford promising him 'upon the word of a king' that he would not suffer 'in life, honour or fortune'. When Parliament sentenced Strafford to death, the

▲ A Dutch print showing the huge crowd present at Strafford's execution

condemned men at once wrote to the King releasing him from his promise. Even so, Charles thought it would be wrong to let him die.

As the King sat in Whitehall palace with the death warrant in front of him, a huge crowd of Londoners armed with swords and cudgels gathered outside. They began to shout 'Justice, justice!' and 'Death to Black Tom Tyrant!' Charles feared that they might break into the palace and injure his family. So in the end, with tears in his eyes, he signed the warrant. He knew he had betrayed Strafford, and he never forgave himself. 'My lord of Strafford's condition is happier than mine,' he said.

Strafford's execution took place on 12 May. He was beheaded on Tower Hill, and as early as 2 a.m. the crowd began to gather. By eleven o'clock, when he was brought out to the scaffold, there were 100,000 people present. Most of them believed that Strafford was to blame for all the quarrels between Charles and his Parliaments, and they thought that after his death all would be well. So when the axe fell, and the executioner picked up Strafford's head and showed it to the crowd, they all cheered. Horsemen rode off to spread the good news shouting, 'His head is off, his head is off!'

Civil War breaks out

In spite of Strafford's death Charles and Parliament continued to quarrel. Parliament did not trust the King. In 1641 a rebellion broke out in Ireland and Parliament voted money to pay an army to restore order. But many MPs feared that Charles might use the army against them, so they demanded that he should hand over control of the army to Parliament. Charles refused. 'By God!' he said. 'Not for an hour.'

Parliament took no notice of the King's refusal. It passed a special 'ordinance' taking over the army without the King's consent. Charles was furious. He left London and went to Nottingham, where he called on all his loyal subjects to join him to fight his disobedient Parliament. The Civil War had begun.

The trial and execution of the King

In the War most Londoners supported Parliament, and the wealth of the city helped Parliament to pay the troops who defeated the King. At the end of the War Charles was captured and brought back to London, where a special court tried him for making war on the people of England. He was found guilty and sentenced to death.

On 30 January 1649, Charles was executed in front of the banqueting hall of his own palace in Whitehall. Young Samuel Pepys was among the crowd. He was a pupil at St Paul's School. He totally approved of the King's execution, and told his schoolmates that if he had to preach a sermon on King Charles I his text would be 'The memory of the wicked shall rot'.

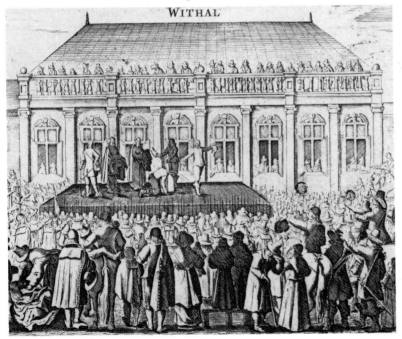

◄ The place where Charles I was executed was carefully chosen. Whitehall was big enough to hold a fair-sized crowd, but small enough to be cleared quickly. The banqueting hall still stands. The rest of Whitehall Palace was burnt down in 1689

Cromwell rules Britain

After the execution of Charles I in 1649, England was ruled by Oliver Cromwell, one of the new commanders of the army which had defeated the King. The Puritans were now in charge. They reformed the Church. There were no bishops. The reformers smashed the statues and stained glass in the churches and forbade the people to celebrate Christmas. They closed all the theatres, and even decreed that anyone swearing should be put in the stocks and pay a fine of three shillings and four pence.

The Puritans were very unpopular, and Cromwell had to rely on his army officers to rule the country. Edward Montagu had fought against the King, and Cromwell knew he could trust him. He made him a member of his Council, and also appointed him General at Sea, an important post in the navy which meant he had to spend several months every summer at sea.

Cromwell's wars

Cromwell used the navy against Holland and Spain. In 1651 Parliament passed the Navigation Act, which said that goods taken to or from England had to be carried in English ships or in ships of the country which had produced the goods. This upset the Dutch. Their ships often carried foreign goods to and from England. They said that the English had no right to pass the Act, and in 1652 the two countries went to war. In 1653 the English defeated the Dutch in three sea battles. The Dutch gave way and made peace in 1654.

Cromwell then sent an expedition to the West Indies to capture the Spanish colony of Hispaniola, so that English merchants could increase trade with the West Indies. The attack on Hispaniola failed. Instead, the expedition captured Jamaica, where English merchants later built up a rich trade in slaves and sugar.

Study

The Civil War

1 (a) Rewrite the events below in chronological order.

   The King refuses to give Parliament control over the army.

   Charles and his Parliament go to war with each other.

   Parliament passes an Act making it impossible for the King to rule without its help and demands the right to punish his ministers.

   Parliament executes Charles for making war on his subjects.

   The King calls Parliament.

   Parliament passes an ordinance taking over control of the army.

   (b) Did the young Samuel Pepys support the King or Parliament?

2 (a) Why did the King need money (i) in 1638, (ii) in 1642?

   (b) What conditions did Parliament make (i) before it would grant the King money in 1638, (ii) after it granted him money in 1642?

   (c) How did the wealth of the Londoners help Parliament to win the war against the King?

3 (a) Look at the picture of Strafford's execution on page 126. Does it give the impression that Strafford's death was popular or unpopular with Londoners? Give reasons for your answer.

   (b) Look at the picture of the execution of Charles I on page 127. Why would the Puritans have chosen a place for the execution that held a fair-sized crowd but that could also be cleared quickly?

Cromwell's army and navy

Read the section on Cromwell on page 128.

1 Copy the sentences below, using these words to fill in the gaps correctly:

navy   army   overseas
Puritans   trading

Cromwell used the officers in his _____ to rule England because the _____ were so unpopular. He built up a strong _____ because he wanted the English to protect their empire _____ and stop other countries from _____ with it.

2 (a) Copy the statement below that is correct:

The Navigation Act said that all goods brought to or taken from England had to be carried either in English ships or in ships of the country that had produced the goods.

The Navigation Act said that goods brought to or taken from England could be carried either in foreign ships or in ships of the country that had produced the goods.

Discussion

Read the section on the Civil War on page 127.

In pairs, answer the questions below:

1 Many people who fought for Parliament thought Charles should give up some of his power. But they still wanted him to be King and believed that it would be wrong to kill him. Why may these people have turned against Cromwell in 1649?

2 In 1642, many MPs had turned against the King when he would not let Parliament control the army that was sent to Ireland to put down the rebellion there. They thought that Charles meant to crush the Irish rebels, and then use the army to make everyone in England obey him. Why may these people have turned against Cromwell when they saw how he used *his* army?

3 Ask one pair to give their answers to the class. Do the rest of you agree?

Pepys's life under Cromwell

In 1650, the year after Charles I was executed, Pepys went to Cambridge University where he studied Greek and Roman philosophy, Latin poetry, mathematics and music. He also learnt how to write shorthand. In 1654 he left Cambridge and returned to London to work for his relation, Edward Montagu.

Pepys's marriage and early career

Montagu was so busy that he had no time to look after his property in London. So he employed Pepys to help him. Pepys had to collect Montagu's salary, pay his bills, make sure that all his servants were doing their jobs properly, and see that his house was kept in good repair.

It was a good job, and in 1655 Pepys, who was now 22, got married. His wife, Elizabeth St Michel, was 15. Her father was a Huguenot who had come to England with Charles I's Queen, Henrietta Maria.

In 1656 or 1657 Montagu got Pepys a job in the civil service. He became a clerk in the exchequer. Every week he had to go for a few hours to the exchequer offices in Westminster, and pay out sums of money as ordered by the officials.

Pepys's stone

The work was not hard, and this was just as well because Pepys was often ill. While he was at Cambridge he had been troubled with a pain in his back caused by a stone in one of his kidneys. In 1653 the stone moved from his kidney and down into his bladder, where it remained for the next five years. Sometimes it lay still, and Pepys was quite comfortable, but occasionally the stone shifted, and caused him such agony that he shouted out.

The pain was always worse when the weather was cold. The winter of 1657–8 was bitter, and Pepys suffered terribly. He decided that rather than live on in misery he would have an operation to remove the stone.

Seventeenth-century surgery

In the seventeenth century very few operations were performed. They had to be done very quickly because there were no anaesthetics, and patients could only bear the agony of being cut with the surgeon's knife for a few minutes. So most surgeons would only pull teeth or amputate limbs.

Even simple operations were likely to lead to the death of the patient because the wounds often went septic. Nobody knew that dirt and germs caused the wounds to fester, so surgeons did not bother to keep the rooms where they did their operations clean, or to sterilise their knives and saws.

Cutting for the stone was a particularly dangerous operation. The shock caused by

▲ This scene is copied from a sixteenth-century engraving of an operation. The patient, who is having his foot amputated, is sitting on a bench

cutting open the abdomen sometimes killed the patient, and even if the stone was removed the wound was very likely to go septic. So when Pepys decided to have the operation he was taking a great risk.

Pepys's operation

Fortunately Pepys's father knew a very good surgeon who agreed to perform the operation. He was Thomas Hollier, and he worked at St Thomas's hospital in London. On 26 March, Hollier cut Pepys open and removed a stone weighing two ounces from his bladder.

The operation was a success. Pepys recovered quickly and by 1 May he was quite better. He never forgot his illness. He kept the stone in a small wooden box, and every year on 26 March he gave a party for his friends to celebrate.

The end of Cromwell's rule

Oliver Cromwell governed the country until his death in September 1658. His son, Richard, then succeeded him as ruler. Oliver had been strong and decisive. But Richard was not interested in politics, and in April 1659 he resigned. A number of army officers took over the government. They were very unpopular, and at the beginning of 1660 General Monck, who commanded a large army in Scotland, brought his troops to London. None of the other generals had enough troops to oppose him.

Monck ordered a new Parliament to be elected. This was done, and the Parliament immediately invited Prince Charles, Charles I's son, to come back from exile in Holland to be king. On 29 May 1660, King Charles II entered London.

Pepys and politics

In August 1658, a month before Oliver Cromwell's death, Pepys and his wife had moved into a house of their own in Axe Yard, Westminster. After Cromwell's death, Pepys became very interested in politics—his cousin, Edward Montagu, was one of the people who helped to arrange Prince Charles's return to England as King.

Study

The King enters London

An engraving of King Charles entering London on 29 May 1660 shows a long procession of soldiers carrying muskets over their shoulders, and standard bearers holding fluttering Union Flags. The King is in the middle of the procession. Four footmen are holding a great canopy over him and the white horse that he is riding. The people of London are standing along the route, waving and cheering to welcome the King home.

Engravings are illustrations printed from a picture that has been cut into a metal or wooden block. They were often used to illustrate the pamphlets that writers published in the seventeenth century to tell everyone what they thought about whatever was going on at the time. By the middle of the seventeenth century, newspapers were also being published in London. Many of them had advertisements, for example, in February 1660 a newspaper called *Mercurius Politicus* advertised a powder for cleaning teeth that was on sale at Thomas Rook's shop near St Paul's Cathedral. The advertisement claimed that the powder 'Preserves from Tooth-ache, fastens the teeth and sweetens the breath.'

In groups of three or four, make the front page of a newspaper that might have been published in June 1660.

1 Divide a large sheet of paper into the sections shown in the diagram opposite. (Do *not* copy the writing on the diagram.)
2 Decide which section of the front page each of you will produce.
3 Cut a piece of writing or drawing paper to fit the section of the front page that you are responsible for and, with the help of the suggestions on the diagram, write or draw your contribution.
4 Mount each contribution carefully onto the large sheet of paper and display your work.

Name of newspaper	
	Date
Report on King Charles entering London	Picture—you might show part of the procession
Interviews with Londoners saying why they are glad or sorry to see the King again. Page 128 may give you some ideas.	Advertisement—you might advertise a shop that specialises in surgical equipment. See page 130 for ideas.

Pepys serves the new King

The new Clerk of the Acts

Charles II was grateful to Edward Montagu, and rewarded him by making him Earl of Sandwich and putting him in charge of the navy. Montagu was delighted at his good fortune. He met Pepys and told him that they would 'rise together'. A few weeks later Pepys heard that he had been appointed Clerk of the Acts to the Navy Board, an important post. He had a salary of £350 a year, two clerks working for him and a fine house in Seething Lane.

In his work Pepys had to inspect dockyards and make sure that the contractors who provided the navy with goods such as timber, ropes and tar were giving good value for money.

At first Pepys knew nothing about the navy,

but he decided to learn. In January 1661 he went to a rope works and 'took great notice' of how cables were made. A month later he bought a 'seaman's grammar and dictionary' to study, so that he would understand all the technical terms the contractors used. In October he persuaded a friendly captain to show him 'every hole and corner' of his ship, and in 1662 he learnt how to measure timber, and found out ways in which contractors cheated the navy and provided less wood than they had promised.

Pepys worked hard. In the summer he was often at his office before eight in the morning, and sometimes worked there until after nine at night. Every Monday morning the Navy Board met at Whitehall palace to organise the next week's work. The king's brother, James, Duke of York, was in charge of the meeting, and Pepys was pleased to find that the duke appreciated his hard work and respected his opinion. In fact Pepys enjoyed his work. 'I find great pleasure in it,' he wrote, 'and a growing contentment.'

▲ Charles II

The court of Charles II

Pepys was very interested in what was going on at court. He met the Duke of York every week at the Navy Board, and found that James took his job very seriously. But King Charles seemed to dislike work. He spent hardly any time with his advisers. His favourite companions were pretty women and idle courtiers who entertained him with witty conversation and stupid pranks. This upset Pepys. 'I know not what will be the end of it but confusion,' he wrote.

Like many others, Pepys underestimated Charles. Though the king was lazy, he was very intelligent, and always did just enough work to prevent 'confusion'. He loved boats. He frequently went sailing and knew how to design ships. He was also very interested in science, and had his own laboratory where he did experiments. In 1685 he spent several days there trying to solidify mercury. He died suddenly a day or two later. Perhaps the mercury fumes poisoned him.

Study

Quakers at court

When Charles escaped to France in 1651 he travelled in a cargo ship called the *Surprise*. On his return to England as King in 1660 he bought the *Surprise* and turned it into a yacht.

The mate of the *Surprise* in 1651 was a man called Carver. He was descended from Deryk Carver, the Flemish Protestant. When the ship beached in the shallows on the French coast, Carver waded ashore with Charles on his back. At that time, Charles could not do much to repay Carver for his loyalty, but he did give him a ring as a token of his thanks.

Carver belonged to The Religious Society of Friends, a group of Christians who were nicknamed 'The Quakers'. These men and women held their services in silence, refused to take part in wars and chose their own leaders. When Charles returned to England, life became difficult for the Quakers, because Parliament passed Acts saying that only people who belonged to the Church of England would be allowed to go to university or hold important jobs. In some parts of the country, Quakers were arrested for holding meetings, so Carver went to Whitehall, showed the King the ring he had once given him, and asked Charles to release them. Charles freed some Quakers, but not as many as Carver hoped he would.

Another Quaker who came to Whitehall was William Penn. His father, Admiral Penn, was a court official and a friend of Pepys. Admiral Penn was worried about his son and at one time William was imprisoned in the Tower of London. But in 1682, after Admiral Penn had died, King Charles gave William permission to set up a Quaker colony in America. William called the colony *Pennsylvania*, or Penn's Woodlands, in memory of his father.

Charles may have felt sorry for the Quakers because he too could not follow his own religion. Like his brother James and several of his courtiers, he was really a Catholic. But he could not say so because if he had, Parliament would not have allowed him to remain King.

▲ A Quaker man and woman

1 (a) Draw the picture of a Quaker woman above.
  (b) What did Quaker men and women refuse to do?
2 (a) Draw the picture of a Quaker man above.
  (b) Which Quaker
      (i) helped Charles to escape to France in 1651,
      (ii) was given permission by Charles to set up a Quaker colony in America?
3 (a) Draw a picture showing
      (i) Charles giving Carver the ring in 1651,
      (ii) Carver showing Charles the ring in 1660.
  (b) Explain why you think Carver showed Charles the ring when he went to see him at Whitehall.

Science and the Royal Society

The Royal Society

Charles II helped to make science fashionable in England. In 1662 he granted a Royal Charter to a group of scientists who used to meet to conduct experiments and discuss their theories. They then became known as the Royal Society. Charles and his brother James, the Duke of York, were both members. So was Pepys. He eventually became President of the Society.

The early experiments: Bacon and Harvey

Before the seventeenth century people did not think that scientific experiments were important. Scholars believed the theories handed down by the Greeks and Romans. If an experiment showed the Greeks to be wrong, then either the scientist's apparatus or his reasoning was faulty. But at the beginning of the seventeenth century Francis Bacon, a famous English lawyer and philosopher, put forward a new idea.

Bacon believed that experiments were vital. He said that doing experiments was the best way to learn, and argued that if the results of the experiments did not agree with the accepted theory, the theory would have to be changed.

Scientists all over Europe began to follow Bacon's advice. Surgeons carefully dissected

bodies and discovered that parts of them were quite unlike what the Greeks had taught. In the Italian town of Padua, William Harvey, an English surgeon, discovered for the first time that blood is pumped all round the body by the heart. He said he had learnt 'not from books, but from dissection'.

Other surgeons learnt from those like Harvey, who dissected bodies and described what they found. When a surgeon cut open a patient to perform an operation, he now knew more about what lay beneath the skin. This made operations like cutting for a stone much safer.

Galileo

The Italian scientist Galileo also worked at Padua. He made many important discoveries. The Greeks had taught that the earth was the centre of the universe. By careful observation with a telescope, Galileo proved that the earth was just a planet revolving round the sun. The Greek philosopher, Aristotle, had said that heavy objects fall more quickly than light ones. Galileo proved that all objects fall at the same speed no matter what their weight.

Boyle and Newton

Members of the Royal Society made important discoveries. Robert Boyle found that air is a substance that can be weighed, and showed that matter is made up of many elements—not just fire, water, earth and air, as the Greeks had said.

The most famous member of the Royal Society was Isaac Newton. He discovered how gravity works. Newton decided that all solid objects attract one another. So the earth attracts falling apples, and the sun attracts the earth and other planets. After long and complicated calculations, he was able to prove that the solar system is held together by this force, which he called the force of gravity.

Newton also found out that white light is made up of a mixture of lights of different colours. He discovered the laws that govern how objects move, and was also a great mathematician.

▲ Scientists at the Royal Society made several experiments in blood transfusion. Here blood is being transfused from a dog into a man

Hopes for the future

By the end of the seventeenth century, scientists had learnt that Bacon was right, and that the best way to learn was to do experiments. They now knew more about the world around them than the philosophers of Greece and Rome had done. They realised that there were still many problems which they had not solved. But they hoped that scientists in the future would find the answers.

▲ The Royal Observatory at Greenwich was founded by Charles II. This room contains a quadrant (left) and a telescope (right)

Study

The movement of heavenly bodies

Galileo and Isaac Newton were both interested in the way in which the planets move in space, and the forces that keep them apart as they follow their paths or orbits. The experiment below will show you something about the laws of motion that these scientists discovered.

Experiment

Put a piece of string through a hole in a large spool. Tie one end of the string to a small spool and the other to a potato. Hold the large spool in your hand and start the smaller spool swinging in a circle overhead. When the small spool is going fast enough, its outward-moving force will lift the much heavier potato.

The same kind of outward force pulls at the moon. But the moon does not fly off into space because the inward pull of gravity keeps it in orbit round the earth.

Pepys and London

Pepys at home

Pepys had no children. He and his wife lived in Seething Lane with two maids and a boy to look after them. Their house belonged to the navy, but Pepys had to keep it in good repair. In 1660 he found that his cellar was flooded with sewage, because the pit into which his neighbour's lavatory emptied had overflowed. Workmen had to empty the pit. Pepys took a pride in his house, and often had workmen in to alter and improve it.

Pepys liked to get up early. In summer he was usually out of bed by four or five in the morning. As a rule he did not have much breakfast—just a drink of ale and a cake—but after a morning's work at the office he expected a cooked dinner to be ready for him about noon. Mrs Pepys and her maid prepared this meal. As a rule they roasted or stewed a joint of meat. Sometimes Pepys went to a tavern for his dinner. His favourite was the King's Head near Charing Cross, where for two shillings and six pence he could eat 'a most excellent neat dinner, and very high company and in a noble manner'.

Sometimes he invited company for dinner. In January 1663, he and his wife entertained six guests to a first course of oysters, followed by 'a hash of rabbits and lamb and a rare chine of beef'. Next there was 'a great dish of roasted fowl and a tart', and the meal ended with fruit and cheese. The feast was, Pepys wrote, 'noble and enough'. It cost him £5, including the wages of a cook specially brought in for the day. This was more than he paid either of his maids for a year's work.

The maids had to work long hours, and so did Mrs Pepys, particularly on washdays. Once in 1660 Pepys was out all day, and came back to find his wife and her maid still doing the washing. He wrote:

> 'I sat up till the bell man came by with his bell, just under my window as I was writing of this very line, and cried "Past one of the clock, and a cold, frosty, windy morning." I then went to bed and left my wife and the maid a-washing still.'

▼ Pepys holding the music of a song he had composed. The portrait was painted when he was thirty-three

Pepys's spare time

After his day's work Pepys liked to relax. He loved music. He could play the viol (a kind of violin), the lute (a sort of guitar) and the flageolet, which was like a flute. He could also sing well. One summer evening in 1661, he sat out in his garden with his neighbour Sir William Penn singing, playing the flageolet and eating fish roe on buttered bread, washed down with 'great draughts' of red wine. They stayed out in the moonlight until after midnight. The next day Pepys had a headache.

Pepys often went to the theatre. He usually saw a new, witty play about fashionable life, but sometimes he went to one of Shakespeare's plays, which were regularly performed. For the first time female parts were played by actresses. Previously boys had performed them.

While he was at the theatre, Pepys's eyes roved round the audience in search of a pretty face. He enjoyed looking at beautiful women, and once when a woman in the theatre turned round in the dark and spat on him 'by mistake' he did not mind, 'seeing her to be a very pretty lady'.

Looking at London

Pepys enjoyed wandering the streets of London, calling in at ale and coffee houses, buying books from the stalls in St Paul's Churchyard, and all the time noticing what was going on.

London streets and houses

When Pepys was born, London had a population of about 400,000. Most of them lived in timber-framed houses over a hundred years old. As a rule each floor overhung the one below, so that at the top the houses almost touched those on the other side of the street.

London's streets were narrow and paved with cobblestones. They had no footpaths, and a single gutter ran down the middle of the road. People flung all the rubbish from their houses into the gutter where it lay, teeming with rats and flies, until the street cleaners swept it up and carried it to the outskirts of the city, where they piled it into great heaps to rot. London stank, and when he walked through the city Pepys always tried to keep well away from the middle of the road.

London was an industrial town, and all the year round the fires of soap-boilers, dyers, brewers and lime-burners pumped out smoke and fumes, while in the winter coal fires in the houses polluted the air. A foreigner wrote that London on a foggy day was like 'a hell upon earth'. He noticed that the dirt in the air left a layer of soot on everything, made people cough and even corroded iron.

London trade and traffic

Most London streets were noisy, busy and crowded. Almost every shopkeeper had an apprentice boy, who stood at his door and tried to attract customers by shouting to the passers-by, telling them the best bargains of the day. Street traders blocked part of the road with their stalls and baskets, while lawyers, business men and housewives picked their way carefully through the mud and filth, and carters pushed their way along with heavily laden wagons pulled by sweating horses.

A huge quantity of traffic came into London. To feed the population, herds of cattle were driven down to the city slaughterhouses, and loads of corn and vegetables were brought in from the country. On the river Thames, colliers from Northumberland and Durham unloaded cargoes of coal, while merchant ships brought goods from America, India and Europe for the London merchants to sell. All these products had to travel through London's narrow streets. To get from one end of London to the other, Pepys found it easier and quicker to take a boat on the river than to struggle through the streets.

▲ Before the Fire many London houses looked like these. In this street, most of the houses had shops on the ground floor

Travel by coach

Sometimes if the streets were very muddy Pepys travelled by coach. Once, while going along a narrow street near Newgate meat market, his coach knocked two pieces of beef down into the mud. Angry butchers immediately surrounded the coach, and claimed that it had done more than £2 worth of damage. But when Pepys gave them a shilling they were 'well contented'.

On another occasion, Mrs Pepys was on her way home in a coach carrying a parcel of clothes she had just bought. When the coach stopped in a traffic jam, a man poked his head in and asked the way to the Tower of London. As she pointed out the road, another man leaned in from the other side and snatched her parcel. Then they both ran away, leaving Mrs Pepys in tears.

Items of interest

In his diary Pepys noted many incidents which caught his interest. When he visited Mr Bland, a London merchant, he was 'pleased to hear Mrs Bland talk like a merchant', and noticed that she understood the business very well. He saw Major General Harrison, one of the court which sentenced Charles I to death, being hanged, drawn and quartered at Charing Cross, 'he looking as cheerfully as any man could do in that condition'.

He saw the parish constable carrying a drunken boy to put him in the stocks, which were 'a new pair and very handsome'. Walking home one night in the dark, he came upon a boy with a lantern looking for rags. He got the boy to light him home, and the lad told him he could sometimes pick up three or four bushels of rags in a day, and sell them for three pence a bushel.

Pepys at church

Pepys went to church at least once every Sunday. Usually he attended his parish church, where there was a pew reserved for the Navy Board. He looked forward to the sermon, but if it was boring he went to sleep.

Occasionally Pepys went to services in the royal chapel at Whitehall, where the King worshipped. Pepys expected the music at Whitehall to be good, but once heard an anthem 'ill sung', which made the King laugh. Charles and his courtiers behaved very badly in church, talking and laughing during the services.

▼ When people were put into the stocks or the pillory, passers-by jeered at them, and sometimes pelted them with stones and rubbish

Study

The London of Samuel Pepys

1 (a) Copy the diagram below onto a double page in your book or a large sheet of paper.
(b) Add two or three pieces of information under headings 2, 3 and 4. (Some information about the Navy Board has already been added.)
(c) Write a heading of your own choice in boxes 5 and 6 and write notes under each heading.

2 Use the information you have gathered to write a paragraph on one or more of the following topics:
    A day in Pepys's life.
    Walking through London.
    Work and pleasure.

3 Use the information that you have gathered to write an essay of three or four paragraphs on: A Day in the Life of a Londoner. Make a list of paragraph headings before you begin to write your essay.

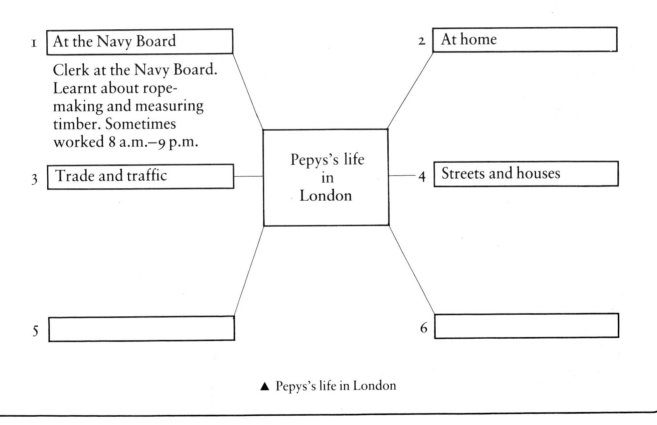

1 | At the Navy Board

Clerk at the Navy Board. Learnt about rope-making and measuring timber. Sometimes worked 8 a.m.–9 p.m.

3 | Trade and traffic

2 | At home

4 | Streets and houses

Pepys's life in London

5 |

6 |

▲ Pepys's life in London

5. Spare Time
6. Interesting Incidents

The Plague of London

Seventeenth-century scientists did not discover what caused diseases, or how to cure them. This was shown clearly by an outbreak of Plague in London in 1665. It began in the spring, and the first cases were in the parish of St Giles-in-the-Fields. There had been many outbreaks of Plague since the Black Death of 1348, and the corporation of London had made strict rules to try to prevent the disease spreading.

Precautions against Plague

When a person died in London the parish clerk had to be told. He then sent the searchers of the dead to examine the body. The searchers, who were two old women, carried white staffs so that everybody would know who they were. They had to decide what had caused the death, and report back to the parish clerk.

If the searchers decided that death was due to Plague, the parish clerk acted at once. Anyone in the house who was ill with Plague was taken to the parish pest house, which was a primitive isolation hospital. Often it consisted of a wooden shed with a few beds and a doctor in charge. The rest of the family were then locked up in their home. Nobody was allowed to go in or out for forty days, and a red cross with the words 'Lord have mercy on us' was painted on the door to warn people to keep away.

Diseases and Casualties this year.

Abortive and Stillborne	617	Executed	21	Palsie	30
Aged	1845	Flox and Smal Pox	655	Plague	68596
Ague and Feaver	5257	Found dead in streets, fields, &c.	20	Plannet	6
Appoplex and Suddenly	116	French Pox	86	Plurisie	15
Bedrid	10	Frighted	23	Poysoned	1
Blasted	5	Gout and Sciatica	27	Quinsie	35
Bleeding	16	Grief	46	Rickets	557
Bloudy Flux, Scowring & Flux	185	Griping in the Guts	1288	Rising of the Lights	397
Burnt and Scalded	8	Hangd & made away themselves	7	Rupture	34
Calenture	3	Headmouldshot & Mouldfallen	14	Scurvy	105
Cancer, Gangrene and Fistula	56	Jaundies	110	Shingles and Swine pox	2
Canker, and Thrush	111	Impostume	227	Sores, Ulcers, broken and bruised Limbes	82
Childbed	625	Kild by several accidents	46		
Chrisomes and Infants	1258	Kings Evill	86	Spleen	14
Cold and Cough	68	Leprosie	2	Spotted Feaver and Purples	1929
Collick and Winde	134	Lethargy	14	Stopping of the Stomack	332
Consumption and Tissick	4808	Livergrowne	20	Stone and Strangury	98
Convulsion and Mother	2036	Meagrom and Headach	12	Surfet	1251
Distracted	5	Measles	7	Teeth and Worms	2614
Dropsie and Timpany	1478	Murthered, and Shot	9	Vomiting	51
Drowned	50	Overlaid and Starved	45	Wenn	1

	Males	5114			Males	48569		
Christned	Females	4853		Buried	Females	48737	Of the Plague	68596
	In all	9967			In all	97306		

Increased in the Burials in the 130 Parishes and at the Pest-house this year———— 79009
Increased of the Plague in the 130 Parishes and at the Pest-house this year———— 68590

▲ Every year a *Bill Of Mortality* was published in London giving the number of deaths in the capital, and showing what caused them. This is the bill for 1665

Everybody hated the idea of being locked up in a house where somebody had just died of Plague, so many people bribed the searchers to say that a Plague victim had died of some other disease. Then the family left the house.

If Plague spread, the authorities took other precautions. They killed all the dogs, forbade all public meetings, and thinking that foul air might cause Plague, they ordered fires to be lit in the street outside every sixth house to purify the atmosphere.

None of these precautions did any good. The rats carrying the fleas which spread the disease easily moved in and out of the locked houses, and with no dogs to kill them, probably increased in number.

The effects of Plague

Throughout the hot dry summer of 1665 the number of deaths from Plague continued to increase, until in September more than a thousand people were dying every day. It was impossible to bury them all properly, and each night the bodies were collected like rubbish in a cart and tipped into pits.

Everybody who could afford to leave London did so. The King and his court went to Salisbury. The merchants and gentry fled into the country. Pepys stayed at his work. He wrote that he could walk along Lombard Street in the city 'and not meet twenty persons from one end to the other'. Probably half London's population left.

Most of those who stayed behind were the poor, who had nowhere else to go. In all about 100,000 of them died. In fact the Plague of 1665 killed about the same proportion of London's population as the Black Death had done more than 300 years earlier.

Pepys's later life

Pepys survived the Plague. He saw London burnt down, and watched as it was rebuilt in brick and stone instead of timber. In 1669, the year he gave up keeping his diary, his wife died. He worked at the Navy Office until 1689. Then he retired, and continued to live peacefully in London until his death in 1703.

▼ A London street at the time of the Plague. The houses have crosses on their doors, fires burn in the road, and dog-killers are at work. Two searchers of the dead with their white sticks walk along the street. Two men carry a Plague victim in a sedan chair to the pest house

▲ This house, in Neville's Court, off Fetter Lane, was one of those built to replace homes destroyed in the Fire of London. The new houses were all made of brick. Timber-frame houses were forbidden. This photograph was taken in 1905. Since then the house has been demolished

Use your imagination

1 Tobias Briggs lives in the parish of St Giles-in-the-Fields. In 1665, when he was a boy, he stayed in London and survived the Plague. Write an account of his life during the Plague year as he might have described it to his grandchildren.

Things to write about:

The work of the parish clerk.

The work of the searchers.

A description of a pest house.

The precautions that the authorities took against the Plague.

(Think of something important that happened to you when you were very young and how it seems to you now.)

2 Women who went out to nurse the sick tried to avoid catching the Plague. They washed their hair in vinegar, sprinkled vinegar on the shawl that they wore over their heads, and held a handkerchief soaked in vinegar to their mouths.

Samantha Thomson is a poor woman who earns money by nursing sick families. Write an account of her visit to a house in Lombard Street in September 1665.

Things to write about:

Her preparations before leaving home.

The houses and death carts she passed as she walked through the streets.

The missing family that she could not find and the reason the searcher gave for the house being empty.

(Think of an event that you have made careful preparations for, only to find that it did not happen.)

3 In the seventeenth century, many houses did not have an oven, so people who had servants sent their maids to the bakehouse with dough to be made into bread or a joint to be cooked. It was thought that maids often caught the Plague when they went to a bakehouse.

Matthew Stephens lives with his family in Pudding Lane, opposite a bakehouse. Each night he records the events of the day in his journal. Write four entries that he might have made between 2 August 1665 and 2 September 1666.

Things to write about:

The precautions Matthew took when he heard there was an outbreak of the Plague in London.

The people he saw coming and going at the bakehouse.

His relief when he heard people in the street saying that the Plague had passed and it was safe to come out.

The flames he saw coming from the bakehouse in the early hours of 2 September 1666.

(Think of something you were afraid of that never happened, and something unexpected that happened when you thought the danger was over.)

The end of the Stuarts

The revolution of 1688

While Pepys was at the Navy Board, England fought two more wars against the Dutch. The fleets of the two countries were evenly matched, and the fighting cost more than King Charles could afford. The two countries finally made peace in 1674, and William of Orange, the ruler of Holland, married Charles's niece, Mary, the daughter of his brother James.

In 1685, when Charles II died, James succeeded him as King. He was a Roman Catholic, and many English politicians believed that he wanted to make England a Catholic country again. So in 1688 they rebelled against James, and he fled to France, where he died in 1701.

When James fled, his daughter and her husband William were invited to come to England from Holland to rule in his place. As James's daughter, Mary ought to have been Queen in her own right, but William would not agree, and in the end they ruled together. Mary died in 1694, and William continued as King until his death in 1702.

The wars against France

William III's home country, Holland, was at war with Louis XIV of France. Louis wanted parts of Holland for himself, and invaded it. When William became king he took England into the war against France, and the two countries spent much of the next hundred years fighting each other, while both tried to build up their overseas empires.

Queen Anne and the Union

William and Mary had no children. After their death Mary's sister, Anne, became Queen. All her children died young, so she was the last Stuart monarch to rule the country.

During the seventeenth century the Stuarts ruled both England and Scotland, but the two countries were still separate. Each had its own law, its own Church and its own Parliament. The English were afraid that when Queen Anne died the Scots might choose their own king. So they decided to make the two countries into one by uniting their Parliaments. This was done in 1707, and they have been united ever since.

▲ A Londoner and his wife

The Stuart dynasty

Dallas

Read the section headed 'The end of the Stuarts' on page 143.

The Stuart dynasty

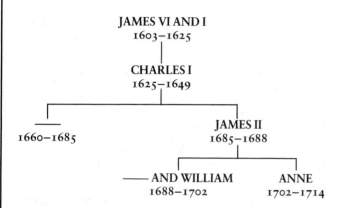

JAMES VI AND I
1603–1625

CHARLES I
1625–1649

——
1660–1685

JAMES II
1685–1688

—— AND WILLIAM
1688–1702

ANNE
1702–1714

From 1649 to 1660 England and Scotland were republics and did not have a king

1 (a) Copy the Stuart family tree.
  (b) Fill in the names of the missing king and queen.
  (c) Why did (i) the King flee to France, (ii) the Queen's husband take England into war against France?
2 (a) Copy the flags opposite.
  (b) Why were the flags of England and Scotland put together in 1606 to form the Union Flag?
  (c) In which year were the Parliaments of England and Scotland united?
3 During the seventeenth century, when the Stuarts ruled Britain, Parliament became more powerful.
  (a) Which king did Parliament
      (i) execute in 1649,
      (ii) agree should return to Britain, on certain conditions, in 1660,
      (iii) invite, with his wife, to rule Britain in 1688?
  (b) Why were the English and Scottish Parliaments united during Queen Anne's reign?

(c) The crowns of England and Scotland were united by the first Stuart to rule Britain. The Parliaments of England and Scotland were united under the last Stuart to rule Britain.
How did the union between England and Scotland that took place in the seventeenth century help the British to build up an empire overseas in the eighteenth century?

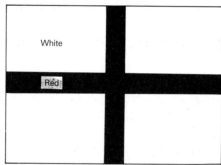

▲ St George's flag, England

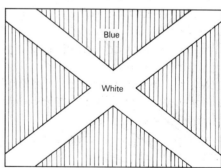

▲ St Andrew's flag, Scotland

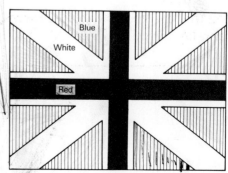

▲ The Union flag, Great Britain, 1606

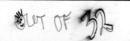

Further work

Writing

1 (a) Write a sentence about each of the following incidents from the life of Samuel Pepys, saying what it shows us about his character. The first sentence has been completed for you.

> Pepys went to tell King Charles how serious the fire was, so he must have had a sense of responsibility.
>
> He forgave a pretty woman who spat on him by mistake...
>
> He was the president of the Royal Society...

(b) Choose two or more things that Pepys said or did and say what each of them tells us about his character.

(c) Write a character study of Charles II.

Drawing

1 (a) Draw a cover for a Puritan pamphlet entitled 'The Theatre—the home of the Devil'.

2 (a) Draw three or four pictures to illustrate street life in London in the seventeenth century. For example, you might show people being punished, or rebuilding the city after the Fire.

(b) Write a sentence under each picture, saying what it shows.

3 (a) Look at the pictures of the man and woman on page 143. Then draw your idea of one of the following:

> A group of Pepys's friends arriving for a dinner party.
>
> King Charles and his courtiers at Whitehall.
>
> London citizens going to church on a Sunday morning.

Oral work

1 (a) Divide the class into seven groups.

(b) Between pages 136 and 138 there are seven descriptions of things that Pepys saw and did around London, beginning with 'Pepys at home' and ending with 'Pepys at church'. Give one section to each group to prepare for a reading.

(c) In your groups, prepare your reading, giving everyone something to read and including sound effects.

(d) Give your reading as a class. If it is good enough, you might record it on tape.

Quiz: When or where?

In what year was Charles I executed?

Where can you still see a church that was burnt but not destroyed in 1666?

In what year did Isaac Newton and other important scientists form the Royal Society?

Make up your own 'When or where?' quiz.

For your glossary

Explain what these words mean, using your own words:

politics   congregation

Library work

Look up the word *Jacobite* under the letter J in an encyclopedia or in the index of a history book on the seventeenth or eighteenth century. Why were the Jacobites given this name? Which family did they think the King of England should belong to?

7 Topic Work

While you have been reading this book, you may have found several topics that you would like to know more about. Writing a topic book gives you a chance to find out more about subjects that interest you.

> *Subjects for topic work*
> You will find information in this book on these topics:
>
> Rebels and Rebellions
> Disease and Doctors
> Flags, Standards and Emblems
> Kings and Queens
> Books and Printing
> Merchants and Traders
>
> Do not decide yet which topic you will write about.

Finding your information

1 *Pictures*
(*In pairs*)
(a) Look at the picture on page 130. Which topic in the list above does this picture illustrate?
(b) Look through the illustrations in this book and find a picture, plan or map to illustrate each of the other topics.

2 *Writing: Using the Index*
By now you are used to using an index. For example, if you wanted to look up *Merchants* you would turn to the letter M. Sometimes you will find useful information listed in an index under a word connected with the title of your project. For example, you might find out something about traders if you looked up *Explorers*.
(*In pairs*)
Write a list of words that you might look up for three of the topics suggested above.

Choosing a topic

1 Choose a topic from the list given above.

2 Draw two or three pictures to illustrate your topic. Write one or two sentences under each picture, explaining what it shows.

3 Using the *Index* to help you, choose *four or more* interesting pieces of information *from at least three sections* of this book. For example, if you choose 'Disease and Doctors' you might write about:
    The Black Death,
    Samuel Pepys's operation,
    The Plague of London.

4 Make notes on the information that you find. For example, the notes below are about an emblem. What do they mean?
    Lancs—red rose

5 *Quotations*
You may use short quotations but you *must* put them in inverted commas. For example, if your topic is going to be about Rebels and Rebellions you might write:
    H told Norf to punish rebs by 'hanging them on trees, quartering them, and setting the quarters in every town'.

6 Use your school and public library to find out more about your topic. Look at the Contents and Index pages of history books, as well as their titles.

7 *When you have gathered your notes and quotations:*
(a) Write an introduction to your topic book, saying why you chose this particular topic and which piece of information that you found out about it surprised or interested you the most. For example, you might have chosen Books and Printing and have been surprised to learn that in Mary's reign ordinary people were not allowed to read the Bible.
(b) Decide in which order you will present your information and write your topic book.

Summing up

Time Chart
Use *a whole page* to make a time chart covering the years 1200 to 1700. Set out your page as shown below.

Date	Important event
1200	
1300	
1400	
1500	
1600	
1700	

Look back over the work that you have done and choose two important events from each century. Fill them in on your time chart.

Famous people
1 Write the names of these famous people in the correct chronological order:
   4 Queen Elizabeth I
   2 Wat Tyler
   5 Samuel Pepys
   1 Robert Bruce
   3 Catherine of Aragon
2 Write a sentence about each of them, saying why he or she is famous.

The British Isles
1 Which King of England
   conquered the Welsh and claimed the overlordship of Scotland,
   signed the Treaty of Northampton in 1328, agreeing that Scotland was an independent country,
   was King of Scotland before he became King of England?
2 Name the two flags that were put together to form the first Union Flag.

Empires overseas
1 Copy the three statements below that are correct.
   Between 1497 and 1600 the Kings and Queens of England:
      Lost their land on the French mainland.
      Claimed territories on the east coast of America.
      Sent settlers to Australia.
      Set up the East India Trading Company to trade with India and the Far East.
2 Why did the English need a strong navy by the end of the sixteenth century?
3 For what reasons connected with trade did the English (a) quarrel with the Spanish before 1588, (b) quarrel with the Dutch after 1588?

Can you spell?
1 Each of the following words has one letter missing:
      Parliment   monastry   negotiatons   confrence
   Rewrite each word, spelling it correctly.
2 Look back through this book and make a list of three names or words that you should be able to spell correctly when you are writing about history. Write each word on a separate piece of paper, give them in and hold a spelling quiz.
3 Make a word-search sheet on Britain, 1200–1700.

Do you understand
   when to make notes,
   why we use quotation marks,
   when to write sentences,
   what a paragraph is?

Look back through your notebook
   Is your work set out clearly?
   Do you understand the work in your notebook?
   Have you learnt the work in your notebook?
Give yourself marks out of ten for your answer to each of the questions above.

Index

Page numbers in **bold** refer to illustrations.

Subjects for topic work are printed in **bold**.